BRAD WHITT

HEROES

AMAZING STORIES OF FAITH

Published by Innovo Publishing, LLC
www.innovopublishing.com
1-888-546-2111

Publishing quality books, eBooks, audiobooks, music, screenplays & courses for the Christian & wholesome markets since 2008.

HEROES
Amazing Stories Of Faith

Copyright © 2024 by Brad Whitt
All rights reserved.

No part of this publication may be reproduced, stored in a retrieval system, or transmitted in any form or by any means electronic, mechanical, photocopying, recording, or otherwise, without the prior written permission of the Author.

All scripture is taken from the New King James Version®. Copyright © 1982 by Thomas Nelson. Used by permission. All rights reserved.

ISBN: 979-8-88928-018-7

Cover Design & Interior Layout: Innovo Publishing, LLC

Printed in the United States of America
U.S. Printing History
First Edition: 2024

Has God called you to create a Christ-centered or wholesome book, eBook, audiobook, music album, screenplay, or online course? Visit Innovo's educational center (cpportal.com) to learn how to accomplish your calling with excellence.

CONTENTS

ABEL: A WORSHIPPING FAITH 7

ENOCH: AN UNDYING FAITH 17

NOAH: A WORKING FAITH 29

ABRAHAM: AN OBEYING FAITH 41

SARAH: A RECEIVING FAITH 53

ISAAC: A FAMILY FAITH 65

JACOB: A PILGRIM FAITH 77

JOSEPH: A VISIONARY FAITH 89

MOSES: A LIBERATING FAITH 101

RAHAB: A SAVING FAITH 115

Unwavering Obedience 125
Additional Books by Dr. Brad Whitt & Innovo Publishing 127

CHAPTER ONE

ABEL: A WORSHIPPING FAITH

Hebrews 11:4; Genesis 4:1-10

In every corner of history, in every culture, and within every heart lies a fascination with heroes—extraordinary individuals who defy the ordinary and embody courage, compassion, and resilience. That's why I've entitled this book *Heroes: Amazing Stories of Faith*. We will journey through biblical stories, exploring the faith of Abel, Enoch, Noah, Abraham, Sarah, Rahab, and others—faith so great that the Holy Spirit chose these individuals as examples of faith. These are heaven's heroes: God's giants of faith.

Hebrews chapter 11 is one of, if not the most significant chapters in the Bible. Many Bible preachers and teachers have described it as God's Hall of Faith. This chapter on faith is famous and foundational because, in these verses, we are provided the definition of faith and given demonstrations of it. In other words, the writer of Hebrews defines what genuine faith is and then goes back to the very beginning of time to give us example after example of mighty men and women of faith.

I want to make this clear: One of the things I love about the Bible is that it presents people just like they were—as the old country saying goes, "warts and all." As we study these heroes of faith, it won't take long for you to see that these weren't perfect people. They not only had great faith, but in many cases, they also had great flaws.

I don't know about you, but that's a real encouragement to me. To see where God took a liar like Abraham, a schemer like Jacob, and a prostitute like Rahab, and despite their flaws and their failings, despite their sin and their shortcomings, He points to them as great examples for us to follow because of their faith.

I'll tell you faith can move mountains; it can turn a sinner into a saint. It can take a man like Moses, who was afraid to speak in front of a crowd, and give him the courage to stand before Pharaoh, the king of Egypt, the most powerful man in the world, and command him to "Let my people go." It can take a selfish, spoiled daddy's boy like Joseph, who was only interested in himself, and change him into the man who not only saved his *family* from famine but an entire nation as well. It can take a ninety-year-old woman like Sarah and cause her to become pregnant and give birth to a son, through whom God would fulfill His promise to Abraham to make his descendants like the stars in the sky or the grains of sand on the seashore. It can take an old preacher like Noah and cause him to spend one hundred years building something that nobody had ever heard of—an ark—for something that had never happened before—a flood—just because God had told him it would happen.

Hebrews 11 begins with these words, "Now faith is the substance of things hoped for, the evidence of things not seen. For by it the elders [that's the folks we're going to be studying] obtained a good testimony. By faith we understand that the worlds were framed by the Word of God, so that

ABEL: A WORSHIPPING FAITH

the things which are seen were not made of things which are visible" (vv. 1-3).

Twenty-four times in the twenty-three verses of Hebrews chapter 11, we find the word *faith*. What is faith? *Faith is hearing, believing, and acting on the Word of God.* Simply put, it's taking God at His Word despite the situation or circumstances. Paul wrote in Romans 10:17, "So then faith comes by hearing, and hearing by the word of God." That's why Paul wrote in 2 Corinthians 5:7, "We walk by faith, not by sight."

As we begin our journey with these giants of the faith, we are first introduced to a man named Abel. The name *Abel* means "breath" or "vanity." Maybe God gave Eve an indication that her second son wouldn't live very long. We don't know, but here's what we do know: even though Abel didn't live a long life, he did live a strong life. And the reason for that was his faith.

The Bible tells us what kind of faith Abel had. The Bible teaches that he had a worshipping faith. Hebrews 11:4 says, "By faith Abel offered to God a more excellent sacrifice than Cain, through which he obtained witness that he was righteous, God testifying of his gifts; and through it he being dead still speaks."

If you turn to Genesis chapter 4, you find where the first couple, Adam and Eve, gave birth to the first brothers, Cain and Abel. You may know the story. One day, Cain and Abel brought their offerings and laid them before the Lord. Cain brought an offering of fruit—tomatoes, squash, beans, corn, all sorts of fruits and vegetables. Abel brought an offering of flesh—a little, perfect, spotless lamb he killed and offered to God. The Bible says God received Abel's offering but rejected Cain's. In Genesis 4, we learn Cain became angry! Moses describes what he did with these vivid words in verse 8, "And it came to pass, when they were in the field, that Cain rose up against Abel his brother, and killed him."

I want to take some time to examine Abel's faith. There's a reason Abel's faith is mentioned first. Through his worship, Abel demonstrated the kind of faith required to fellowship with God. This chapter contains several principles I want you to consider as we contemplate what it means to have a worshipping faith. The following is the first and most foundational principle:

GOD ACCEPTS OUR WORSHIP WHEN OUR WORSHIP IS ACCEPTABLE

Hebrews 11:4 tells us, "Abel offered to God a more excellent sacrifice." Genesis tells us that God respected or received Abel's offering but rejected Cain's. In the Bible, offerings and sacrifices are pictures of worship; therefore it's evident we're being taught something about worship.

If you want to understand what life is about, then you must understand worship. Worship is the beginning and the basis for understanding the greatest question that man has ever asked: *Why am I here?* The answer? You were created for worship.

If you don't understand the importance of worship, if you don't understand the importance of having a right relationship with the God of the universe, then you don't understand what life is about. Jesus tells us in Mark chapter 12 that the first and greatest commandment is to love the Lord with all our heart, soul, mind, and strength. In other words, you must love and worship Him with everything you have.

One day, thousands of years ago, two brothers came to worship God. The Bible indicates that there was a specific place, a specific period of time, and a specific plan they were to follow when they came to worship God. No doubt, Adam and Eve had shared with their sons what it was like to worship with God before the fall and how sweet it was literally to walk with Him through the garden. But sin had come into the world, and with sin came separation, which created a marked difference in their worship that hadn't existed before the Fall.

Cain brought his offering, and Abel brought his offering. But here's the question: *Why did God receive Abel's worship but reject Cain's?* Or, to put it more personally, *How can we be sure*

ABEL: A WORSHIPPING FAITH

God accepts us? Because here's the thing: God didn't just reject Cain's offering; He rejected Cain.

God didn't just accept Abel's offering; He accepted Abel. Warren Wiersbe, Christian pastor and author, says it wasn't Cain's offering that was rejected; it was Cain himself who was rejected because of his callous heart toward God.[1]

What's the difference between being accepted or rejected by God? Here's the difference: you've got to come to God on His terms, not yours. Cain tried to come to God on his terms, not God's. He thought that he could work the ground and, through his works, produce something acceptable. But the Lord had already said the ground was cursed. There was nothing that Cain could grow, nothing that he could do that would be good enough to offer as a sacrifice for his sin.

That's the mistake many people make, and maybe some of you reading this have also made that mistake. You've thought you could try to live a moral life. You've thought you could try to be a good person. You've felt you could go to church and give and serve and somehow through your works produce something that would be acceptable to God.

However, the Bible says in Isaiah 64:6, ". . . all our righteousness is like filthy rags." Titus 3:5 tells us "it's . . . not by works of righteousness which we have done, but according to His mercy He saved us, through the washing of regeneration and renewing of the Holy Spirit."

If you're going to come to God, you've got to come on His terms or not at all. And His terms are *really* simple. You've got to come through the blood. Cain learned quickly that you can't get blood from a turnip. Abel had heard God's Word and heeded God's Word. He brought to God not a bloodless sacrifice but a bloody sacrifice. That's how you come to God. It's through the blood. Leviticus 17:11 tells us, "It is the blood that makes atonement for the soul."

---

1. Warren Wiersbe, "The Worshipper (4:3-7)" from *Warren Wiersbe BE Bible Study Series*. Copyright © Warren W. Wiersbe. Generously provided by David C. Cook.

You've got to come through the blood, and you've also got to come by faith. Ephesians 2:8-9 says, "For by grace you have been saved through faith, and that not of yourselves; it is the gift of God, not of works, lest anyone should boast." That's what Abel did, and that's why God accepted him. He didn't try to come on his own merit but through God's mercy. He didn't try to come through the works of his hand; he went through the blood of the lamb. He came on God's terms, not his terms, and God accepted him and his worship.

That's an excellent lesson for us to learn as believers. We not only have to be saved by faith; we also must serve by faith. In our worship and walk, we must come to God on His terms, not ours. God's Word says, "whatever is not from faith is sin" (Romans 14:23). If I stand up to preach more confident in my ability than I am of His authority, it's sin. If those in worship ministry stand up to sing more confident of their own abilities than of God being able to touch a heart, it's sin. If a deacon tries to minister or care for his church body based on his personality instead of the Person of the Holy Spirit, it's sin. Teachers, if you stand before your class to teach and you're more impressed with your ability to speak than you are with the Word's ability to teach, it's sin. If you try and raise your children by the baby book instead of God's Book, it's sin. If you try to work apart from faith, witness apart from faith, walk apart from faith, give apart from faith, or serve apart from faith, the Bible says that is sin.

God accepts our worship when our worship is acceptable.

RIGHT WORSHIP BECOMES A WITNESS OF RIGHTEOUSNESS

That's precisely what Hebrews 11:4 says: "By faith Abel offered to God a more excellent sacrifice than Cain, through which he obtained witness that he was righteous, God testifying of his gifts."

I want you to catch that because it is very important. Abel wasn't made righteous through the giving of that offering. The giving of that offering showed that he was righteous. That's what

ABEL: A WORSHIPPING FAITH

the word *witness* means: "to testify" or "to show." Abel witnessed through his righteous worship, and God testified that Abel and his worship were indeed righteous.

Let's understand what worship is. There's a lot of misunderstanding today about what worship is. Most people think worship is singing. Many people think worship is praying. There are a lot of people who think worship is going to church on Sunday morning and "clocking in" for God. But worship is so much more than any of those things could ever be.

Do you want to know what real worship is? Real worship is a life lived for God. It is a life given to the Lord. Why do you think God commands that we give Him the first day of every week and the first dime out of every dollar? Do you believe God, the One who created time, the same One who created the world and everything in it, is desperate for our time and money? No. That's not what God desires. God desires you. God doesn't need your time; He wants you. God doesn't need your money; He wants you. God doesn't need your ability or personality; He wants you. He loves you and longs for fellowship with you. Giving of time and money are just ways you and I can show the Lord and the world that we understand everything we are and that everything we have belongs to Him.

The Bible says, "Abel brought a more excellent sacrifice." Genesis 4:4 says Abel brought "the firstborn of his flock and of their fat." God deserves the first, and God deserves the best.

As Dr. Stan Coffey and I were talking one day, he said something that got my attention: "You know, Brad, so many people expect the church of God to operate on spare time and pocket change."[2] When you give God the first and bring God your best out of a willing, cheerful, faithful heart, it is a powerful witness of righteousness. That's why James, the half-brother of Jesus, said in 2:18, "But someone will say, 'You have faith, and I have works.' Show me your faith without your works, and I will show you my faith by my works."

---

2. Dr. Stan Coffey, in a personal conversation. Date unknown.

You say, "But Pastor, that's contradictory." No, it's complimentary. Right worship becomes a witness of righteousness.

JUST BECAUSE THE LORD RESPECTS YOUR WORSHIP DOESN'T MEAN THE WORLD WILL

That's exactly what the Bible teaches. As a matter of fact, Jesus even gave us a warning. He said in John 15:20, "If they persecuted Me, they will also persecute you." And He explained why. "A servant is not greater than his master."

The Bible says that if Jesus suffered, we will suffer. If Jesus was ridiculed, we will be ridiculed. If Jesus was rejected, we will face rejection. If Jesus was persecuted, we will be persecuted. Second Timothy 3:12 says, "Yes, and all who desire to live godly [that means to live a life of worship and witness] in Christ Jesus will suffer persecution." I feel many people today are willing to accept the fact that Jesus suffered for their sins, but they are not willing to accept the fact that they might have to suffer for the Savior.

In Genesis chapter 4, the Bible tells us the result of the rejection of Cain's worship and the reception of Abel's worship. Cain became angry, and the Bible says that while he and his brother were in the field, he rose up against Abel and killed him. Consider these questions: Who was Cain angry with? Was he angry with Abel? Yes. But even more than that, he was mad at God. The 20th-century German theologian Dietrich Bonhoeffer asked, "Why does Cain murder?" His answer was, "Out of hatred for God."[3]

Just because the Lord respects your worship doesn't mean the world will.

---

3. Dietrich Bonhoeffer, taken from *Genesis: Beginning and Blessing* by Kent R. Hughes, © 2012, p. 105. Used by permission of Crossway, a publishing ministry of Good News Publishers, Wheaton, IL 60187, www.crossway.org.

ABEL: A WORSHIPPING FAITH

EVEN THOUGH YOU ARE MORTAL, YOUR WITNESS ISN'T

Hebrews 11:4 ends with these powerful words, "Through it [through what? His righteous worship and his subsequent murder—dying for his faith] he being dead still speaks."

Do you want to live beyond yourself? Then live a life of worship. Through your worship, a witness will live on throughout the years. Perhaps you've heard someone talking about a godly mother or father or grandmother or grandfather, saying something like this, "They knew God. They loved God. They served God. They walked with God." They may have been dead for twenty, thirty, forty, or even fifty years, but their witness lives on. I don't know about you, but I want to outlive myself. I want my sermons to keep preaching, reaching, and teaching people long after I've died.

That's what Abel's sermon did. You did know that Abel was a preacher and a prophet, didn't you? Luke 11 tells us he was a prophet, and his one sermon is still preaching, reaching, and teaching today.

Dietrich Bonhoeffer, the great German theologian and pastor I quoted earlier, stood for the Jews and against the Nazis in 1940s Germany. He helped create a new group called "the confessing church" and led an "illegal seminary." He was arrested and hung in 1945. With his dying breath, he said that this was only the beginning of his life. "He, being dead, still speaks" (Hebrews 11:4). Why? Because through his faith, Abel's sacrifice was greater.[4]

Let me share something as we end this chapter: Faith and worship always go together. You must have faith in the God you worship, and you will only worship the God you have faith in.

---

4. Dietrich Bonhoeffer, in James C. Howell, *Introducing Christianity: Exploring the Bible, Faith, and Life* (Louisville, KY: Westminster John Knox Press, 2009), 66.

CHAPTER TWO

ENOCH: AN UNDYING FAITH

Hebrews 11:5-6; Genesis 5:21-24; Jude 14-15

Hebrews 11 provides us with the definition and demonstrations of real faith. And if you'll recall, in the last chapter, I shared with you a simple working definition of biblical faith: Faith is hearing, believing, and acting on God's Word. It is trusting God despite your situation or circumstances.

The Bible says, "Faith comes by hearing and hearing by the Word of God" (Romans 10:17). The Bible also says that we are to "walk by faith and not by sight" (2 Corinthians 5:7). The world says, "Seeing is believing," but the Word says, "No, believing is seeing." That's why Hebrews chapter 11 begins by stating, "Now faith is the substance of things hoped for, the evidence of things not seen" (v. 1).

In this book, we are simply walking our way down through these mighty men and remarkable women of faith. These are heaven's heroes: God's giants of the faith. Dr.

Warren Wiersbe said we must keep company with faithful friends to increase our faith.[5] And that's what we're going to do in Hebrews 11. We're going to walk with giants of the faith.

We will worship with Abel, walk with Enoch, and work with Noah. We'll witness in all of these other folks just what kind of faith it takes to get from earth to heaven—or maybe just as importantly, what kind of faith it takes to experience a little bit of heaven here on earth.

As we read verse 5, we are introduced to Enoch. Enoch's name means "dedicated one" or "consecrated one." In other words, he was a man who was "sold out" for God. Here's what Hebrews 11:5 has to say about his faith: "By faith, Enoch was taken away so that he did not see death, and was not found, because God had taken him; for before he was taken he had this testimony, that he pleased God."

If you go back to the very first book in the Bible, the book of Genesis, and begin reading about Enoch, this mighty man of faith, in chapter 5, you will discover two things immediately. First, according to the Bible, Enoch is one of only two men who "walked with God." Others may have walked before God or after God or in the presence of God, but only Enoch and Noah are said to have literally, spiritually, and intimately walked with God. R. Kent Hughes wrote that Enoch's "walk was rooted in deepest intimacy with God; he knew God."[6]

Second, if you were to keep reading, you would discover that Enoch is one of only two men ever to live but never die. Genesis 5:24 says, "Enoch walked with God, and he was not, for God took him."

In 2 Kings 2:11, the Bible says Elijah and Elisha were walking and talking together when "suddenly a chariot of fire

---

5. Warren Wiersbe, sermon, source unknown.
6. Taken from *Genesis: Beginning and Blessing* by Kent R. Hughes, © 2012, p. 121. Used by permission of Crossway, a publishing ministry of Good News Publishers, Wheaton, IL 60187, www.crossway.org.

appeared with horses of fire and separated the two of them; and Elijah went up by a whirlwind into heaven." Enoch and Elijah never had to walk through the valley of the shadow of death. They walked in the light of God's love right into the very throne room of God.

A father and his young son were walking along a beach one day when they saw a dead seagull lying on the beach. The son asked his dad what had happened. The father wanted to begin to explain about death and dying, so he gently began to say, "Well, he flew up to heaven." The son said, "And God threw him back?"

The Bible says that Enoch flew up to heaven, but God didn't throw him back. Instead, He placed him in the greatest gallery of faith in the Bible.

What kind of faith did Enoch possess? Enoch had an undying faith. He lived for God, he walked with God, and because of his unwavering faith, he never died. That right there makes him a hero of the faith. His faith allowed him to do something that has only been done one other time in human history.

There are several things that we can learn from walking with this hero of the faith named Enoch.

AN ORDINARY LIFE CAN BECOME AN EXTRAORDINARY LIFE

Look in Genesis chapter 5, beginning in verse 21, because there is something here that you'll miss if you're not careful. The Bible says, "Enoch lived sixty-five years and begot Methuselah." Just stop right there.

For sixty-five years, there was nothing special about Enoch's relationship with God. For sixty-five years, there was nothing different, nothing distinctive, about his walk. His record begins just like the six other names listed before him. "Enoch lived sixty-five years, and he begot Methuselah," but "after he begot

Methuselah, Enoch walked with God three hundred years, and had sons and daughters" (Genesis 5:22).

The turning point in Enoch's life didn't come at twenty-five, or thirty-five, or forty-five, or even fifty-five years of age. Enoch began to walk with God when he was sixty-five years old.

There's an important lesson for us right there. The Bible doesn't say that "Enoch lived sixty-five years, and he started drawing Social Security, and he died." That's not what it says at all. The Bible says that Enoch didn't even start living until he was sixty-five.

There are some of you out there, and the devil has told you, "Well, you're old now, and you're used up, and you can't do anything for God." You know what? If you're retired, you've got more time to serve Jesus than ever before.

Enoch lived sixty-five years, and then he moved next to an elementary school and started having kids. Now there's a man with a vision. And the very first kid that Enoch had was a boy by the name of Methuselah.

Who was Methuselah? That's right; he was the oldest man who had ever lived. Methuselah lived for almost a millennium; he lived 969 years, and somehow, some way, for some reason, the birth of that little baby totally changed Enoch's life.

I've seen that over and over again as a pastor. A couple dates in high school, maybe they go to church, and maybe they don't. They get married, and they get busy. Church doesn't seem to be much of a priority to them anymore, and they walk away from God. But then they find out they're pregnant. They discover they're going to have a baby, and suddenly, they begin to look at the world they live in and walk in. They decide they don't want to raise their baby in that kind of world. So they get back to church, and they draw near to God, and they begin to walk with God afresh and anew.

I'll tell you, one of the greatest life lessons I've learned is that nothing increases your faith in God like having a baby. I mean, when you begin to think about holding that baby, feeding that baby, and raising that baby, or heaven knows, changing that baby's dirty diapers, you know that you're going to need help from heaven. Amen?

One day, shortly after the birth of their new baby, the mother had to go out to do some errands, so the proud father stayed home to watch his wonderful new son. Soon after the mother left, the baby started to cry. The father did everything he could think of, but the baby just wouldn't stop crying. Finally, the dad got so worried he decided to take the infant to the doctor. After the doctor listened to all the father had done to stop the baby's crying, the doctor began to examine the baby's ears, chest, and then down to the diaper area. When he opened the diaper, he found it was indeed full.

"Here's the problem," the doctor explained. "He just needs to be changed."

The perplexed father remarked, "But the diaper package specifically says it's good for up to ten pounds!"

So, when this baby was born, it marked a turning point in Enoch's life. The Bible says it was when Methuselah was born that Enoch began to walk with God. Now, why would the birth of this baby be such a big deal that it would forever change his relationship with God? I think the answer to that question is found in what the name *Methuselah* means. Some have interpreted the name of Methuselah to mean "when he dies, it will come." What will come? The flood.

When Methuselah died, the flood came. That's why Methuselah lived so long. God kept on prolonging Methuselah's life and pushing back his death to put off the judgment of that fatal flood. Isn't that just like the Lord?

We read in 2 Peter 3:9, "The Lord is not slack concerning His promise, as some count slackness, but is longsuffering toward us, not willing that any should perish but that all should come to repentance."

Our God is a good God. He doesn't want anyone to perish. He doesn't want anyone to die and go to hell. So He allowed Methuselah to live for almost a thousand years to give this wicked world more time to repent. Maybe the Lord told

Enoch this truth after that baby was born, and it so gripped and grabbed Enoch's heart he began to walk with God and do God's will.

I want to make sure that you understand this one point, and we'll move on. It wasn't the birth of that baby that transformed Enoch's ordinary life into an extraordinary life. That's just what the Lord used to get his attention. What totally transformed his life was his walk with the Lord. Enoch walked with God.

Let me tell you something, folks. When you begin to walk with God, it's not just a change of space; it's a change of spirit. It's not a new road; it's a new reality. That's what makes it so great.

Enoch was still working, witnessing, and walking just like he had before. He was still fixing the house, talking to his friends, and raising those kids, but when he began to walk with God, he did the same old things with a brand-new life and love and light. He worked with a different strength. He witnessed with a new love. He walked down the same road he'd walked the day before, but yesterday he'd walked alone, and today he walks with God! That simple faith transformed his ordinary life into an extraordinary life.

A LIVING FAITH IS AN UNDYING FAITH

This is the classic statement on the faith of Enoch. Here's the result and the reward of his walk of faith: "Enoch walked with God; and he was not, for God took him" (Genesis 5:24).

Enoch walked by faith, and he "was not" by faith. Instead of entering a tomb, he experienced a *translation*! God did something new, something He had never done before but definitely will do again at the rapture of the church. He reached down and took a man, body and all, straight into heaven. Enoch went to heaven without having to die.

That really is amazing when you consider the context of Genesis 4 and 5. You see, there were only two kinds of people on the earth in the days of Enoch. There were the descendants of Cain and the descendants of Seth. Cain's kin are listed in Genesis 4, and the sons of Seth are listed in Genesis 5. Cain's kind lived for this world, but Seth's kind lived for the world to come.

Genesis 4 tells us about Cain's kind. The Bible says that they were socially permissive, scientifically progressive, but spiritually presumptuous. To record Cain's kind of people, the Holy Spirit takes us into big, bustling cities—cities full of excitement and activity, where everywhere you look there is the hustle and bustle of life.

But in Genesis 5, when we read about Seth's kind, we aren't taken to a noisy city but to a quiet cemetery. Over and over in Genesis chapter 5, we read these words: "And he died . . . and he died . . . and he died . . . and he died . . . and he died . . . and he died." Wait a minute, why in the world would the Holy Spirit do that? Why would God use that phrase over and over and over again? I'll tell you why. He's proving the devil to be the liar that he is. The devil had told Seth and Cain's mother, "You will not surely die." But God said, "He died . . . he died . . . he died."

There's something eternally important in this chapter I don't want you to miss. The Holy Spirit says twice about each of these godly men—they "lived." "He lived . . . he lived . . . he died." The Bible doesn't say that about Cain's kin. Why is that so eternally important? Because each one of Seth's sons experienced a birth and another birth. Each lived and lived on, living again on the other side of the new birth. Jesus told Nicodemus in John 3:3, "I say to you, unless one is born again, he cannot see the kingdom of God." He said in John 10:10, "I have come that they may have life and that they may have it more abundantly." So, from heaven's vantage point, it wasn't the Cainites with their busy, bustling cities who really lived; it was the quiet, unassuming Sethites, those who didn't give in to the world's pleasure, prosperity, or power, who really lived.

But then, right in the middle of all these graves is a man who didn't die. Enoch lived, and he lived again, but he didn't die. Enoch was taken up from this earthly life and transformed for eternal life. He was exempted by God from the law of death and decay to serve as an example for the faithful who will be alive when Jesus comes again. Because on that day, just as it was with Enoch,

> *This corruptible must put on incorruption, and this mortal must put on immortality. So, when this corruptible has put on incorruption, and this mortal has put on immortality, then shall be brought to pass the saying that is written: "Death is swallowed up in victory. O Death, where is your sting? O Hades, where is your victory?" The sting of death is sin, and the strength of sin is the law. But thanks be to God, who gives us the victory through our Lord Jesus Christ. (1 Corinthians 15:53-57)*

Jesus said, "He that lives and believes in Me, shall never die" (John 11:5). A living faith is an undying faith.

OUT OF SIGHT DOESN'T MEAN OUT OF MIND

Hebrews 11:5 says, "By faith, Enoch was taken away so that he did not see death, and was not found, because God had taken him." In other words, people missed him, and they went looking for him. God reached down and grabbed Enoch, and suddenly, they realized the worth of a man who knew how to walk with God. Enoch walked with God, and God took him. There was a tremendous sense of loss that swept throughout his home, his community, where he worked, and where he worshipped. And they went to look for him, but they couldn't find him because God had taken him.

Today, if there is somebody who really walks with God, the world will despise them. They may even be disliked by those around them who know God but don't walk with God. They'll talk about him: "You know, I like old John, but he just expects too much. He needs to get with the times. He really needs to loosen up a little bit. Did you know he actually reads his Bible and prays every single day? Did you know he actually thinks we ought to be at church Sunday morning and Sunday night? Did you know he actually thinks tithing still applies today? Did you know he thinks we ought to be telling the folks we work with and hang out at the ballpark about Jesus? He even thinks he's too good to have a beer with us. I'll tell you; I don't know who he thinks he is, but it's getting to where I don't like being around him."

I'm sure they said those kinds of things—and worse—about Enoch, but once he was gone, he was missed by both sinner and saint alike. As a matter of fact, he was missed so much that they looked everywhere for him but couldn't find him because God had honored his faith, translated him, and taken him to heaven.

IF YOU PLEASE GOD, IT DOESN'T MATTER WHOM YOU DISPLEASE

I don't care what you say; that point preaches for itself. If you please God, it doesn't matter who you displease. Hebrews 11:5 says, "For before he was taken, he had this testimony, that he pleased God." Enoch was pleased to walk with God, and his walk was pleasing to God. As a result, Enoch wasn't just missed by those around him; he was marked by those around him. During his lifetime, men marked him out as a man whose life and testimony were godly. That was the force of his faith; his life had an impact on people.

David Livingstone was one such man. He gave his life to the pursuit of three major objectives: exploring, evangelizing, and emancipating. He opened Africa to the gospel and struck a blow against the devilish slave trade, but, above all, he won people to Christ. During his lifetime, he was often criticized because of his unswerving devotion to these goals. He was bitterly denounced for leaving his wife and children behind as his path took him into dangerous places. But his worth was well known by others, and honors were heaped upon him for his discoveries. He made a mark upon his time. Then, upon his death, his body was brought home to England to be buried in Westminster Abbey, England's national shrine for the greatest of her dead. On the day of his funeral, one of England's best-read papers blazed forth this banner headline: "Granite May Crumble, But This Is Living Stone!"[7]

So how can you and I walk in such a way that we are pleasing to God? How can we, as Paul wrote in Ephesians 5:15, "walk circumspectly, not as fools but as wise"? How can we have a wise walk? Look at the next verse in Hebrews 11—verse 6, "But without faith it is impossible to please Him, for he who comes to God must believe that He is, and that He is a rewarder of those who diligently seek Him."

The writer of Hebrews gives us three statements about pleasing God: There's the great impossibility, "Without faith it is impossible to please God"; there's the great imperative, "for he who comes to God must believe that he is . . ."; there's the great incentive, "and that He is a rewarder of those who diligently seek Him" (Hebrews 11:6).

Enoch received his reward and became the first to live and never to die. Enoch lived in a day, much like the day in which you and I live, days surrounded by gloom. And he received, just like many of us have, saving grace. But because of his simple goodness, walking with God, he experienced a sudden glory. One moment, he was here, and the next, he was there, walking in his own body down the streets of gold.

James Stuart Bell shared his thoughts on how Enoch went to heaven: "Enoch walked with God and simply

---

7. David Livingstone, taken from *Exploring Hebrews: An Expository Commentary*, p. 153 © Copyright 1988 by John Phillips. Published by Kregel Publications, Grand Rapids, MI. Used by permission of the publisher. All rights reserved.

disappeared into heaven one day. . . . [O]n that day the Lord said, '[Enoch], we're a lot closer to my house than yours. Why don't you just come home with me?'"[8] And he did. He took one step on earth and the next in heaven. That is an undying faith.

---

8. Some content taken from *The One Year Men of the Bible: 365 Meditations on the Character of Men and Their Connection to the Living God* by James Stuart Bell, p. 9. Copyright © 2008. Used by permission of Tyndale House Publishers. All rights reserved.

CHAPTER THREE

NOAH: A WORKING FAITH

Hebrews 11:7; Genesis 6–7

In this series of studies, we are determining just what kind of faith Abel had, what kind of faith Enoch and Noah and Abraham and Sarah and Isaac and Jacob and Moses and Rahab had, which caused the Lord to place them into this great listing of the heroes and heroines of the faith. Evidently, there was something unique and special about their faith, which caused them to be selected and pointed to as examples of great faith for us to follow today.

That's why the Bible says in 1 Corinthians 10:11, "all these things happened to them as examples, and they were written for our admonition, upon whom the ends of the ages have come." We are then reminded in verse 13, "no temptation has overtaken you except such as is common to man; but God is faithful."

As we study the lives of these great men and women of the faith, make sure you understand two things: First, the times they lived and walked in weren't all that much different than the times you and I live and walk in today. People are still people; they had many of the same temptations and frustrations that we have today. Second, the reason for their great faith is that they trusted, ultimately, in the faithfulness of God Himself. That ought to be a great encouragement to you today—to know God is the same and never changes because He's "the same yesterday, today, and forever" (Hebrews 13:8); you and I can exhibit and experience great faith because "God is faithful" (1 Corinthians 10:13).

Before we get too far into this chapter, I want us to think about Halloween, a day marked on the secular calendar as the day when kids, both big and little alike, dress up in silly or scary costumes and go asking for tricks or treats. Of course, I heard about a man who got beat up at a Halloween party last year. He went as a piñata.

Now, I'm not going to say too much about Halloween except to say this: as a Christian, you really have no business celebrating a holiday that promotes demons and devils and ghosts and goblins and witches and warlocks and all of these other demonic sort of things because, by doing so, you may be unknowingly inviting demons into your home and into the life of your family. You say, "Aw, Pastor, it's harmless." No, it's hellish, and the Bible says you're not supposed to play around with mediums and familiar spirits and those kinds of things, or you'll be defiled by them. Keep that in mind when you're dressing your little ones up as a witch or warlock or a ghost, goblin, devil, or demon. It really isn't child's play.

You know that October 31 is Halloween on the secular calendar, but what you may not know is that October 31 is a very important day on the *sacred* calendar as well. You see, for those of us who believe and love the Bible, it's the anniversary of the beginning of what is known as the Protestant Reformation.

On October 31, 1517, Martin Luther, a Catholic priest, had been studying his Bible. He read Habakkuk 2:4, "The just shall live by faith." Disquieted, Luther nailed a list of concerns and convictions to the door of the church in Wittenberg, Germany. That list, referred to by most folks today as "The 95 Theses," was a direct challenge to the Catholic Church's doctrine and declaration that the pope could forgive sins by selling what were called *indulgences*. So, Martin Luther, after reading and believing the Word of God, became so convicted and convinced that what the Catholic Church was teaching and doing was wrong he was willing to challenge the authority of the pope himself.

The pope issued a statement threatening Luther with excommunication—being kicked out of the church—if he didn't retract his statement and quit teaching his beliefs. Luther received the letter on October 10 and publicly burned it on December 10. Consequently, the pope excommunicated him. All came to a head in March when Emperor Charles V summoned Martin Luther to Worms, Germany, to defend himself. At his trial, he was publicly asked if he would "recant" or "retract" what he had written, to which he said, "Here I stand, I can do no other." So, on May 8, 1521, Martin Luther was placed under an Imperial Ban and excommunicated from the Catholic Church, birthing the Protestant Reformation. A preacher believed the Word of God and took a hammer and a nail and, through his faith and work, totally changed the world.

Thousands of years ago, there was another preacher who believed the Word of God, and just like Martin Luther, he took a hammer and some nails, and, through his faith and through his work, he brought about a worldwide *reformation*.

His name was Noah, and the Bible tells us about Noah and his faith in Hebrews chapter 11. Verse 7 says that "by faith Noah, being divinely warned of things not yet seen, moved with godly fear, prepared an ark for the saving of his household, by which he condemned the world and became heir of the righteousness which is according to faith."

Noah's name means "rest" or "comfort," and that's almost amusing when you consider that Noah is best known for his one hundred years of building the ark and a flood that destroyed the entire world.

You know the story. God chose to send a flood and destroy the world. God told Noah to build an ark, and for one hundred and twenty years, Noah gathered, sawed, hammered, and sealed wooden planks together into the boat that God had told him to build.

When the boat was ready, God told Noah to gather the animals and bring them in two by two into the ark. When everybody was on board, God shut the door and sent the flood, which destroyed the world with water. For forty days and forty nights, Noah and his ark floated on those flood waters until the waters subsided and the ark came to rest on dry ground.

Most, if not all, of us know that story. We've heard it all our lives. Like Abel and Enoch, the two men mentioned before Noah in Hebrews chapter 11, there is so much more to Noah's faith and example than the simple story that I just shared with you. What we have is a fantastic account of a man who believed God, walked with God, and worked for God for hundreds of years, and in spite of the facts, he walked by faith.

All right, let's look at the life of Noah, and let me share with you several things we can learn about a faith that works.

YOU CAN WALK WITH THE LORD IN A WICKED WORLD

To understand the context of Hebrews chapter 11, you must go all the way back to Genesis. In Genesis chapter 6, what you'll find is a wicked world and a perverted planet. There, in the first five verses, you find marriage was demonized, life was minimized, and violence was idolized.

Genesis 6:1-2 says,

> *Now it came to pass, when men began to multiply on the face of the earth, and daughters were born to them [Evidently there was a population explosion. Men began to multiply, and the great growth of that population led from a spiritual decay to a shameless depravity because in*

that next verse it says . . .], that the sons of God saw the daughters of men, that they were beautiful; and they took wives for themselves of all whom they chose.

There is a great deal of debate as to what's taking place here. Some Bible scholars believe that when Scripture refers to "the sons of God," it's talking about fallen angels—demons, if you will. And so, here you have demons taking the form of men and marrying "the daughters of men" and creating a race of giants (verse 4) who create great conflict and chaos on the earth. There is some support for this idea. For one thing, every other time in the Old Testament, when the phrase "beth-elohim" or "the sons of God" is used, it refers to angels. In the New Testament, in 2 Peter, the angels who sinned and Noah are mentioned in the same context.

Then there are those Bible scholars on the other side who say, "No, these weren't fallen angels; these were the sons of Seth who compromised with this world and disobeyed the commands of God and began to marry into the sinful line of Cain, thus placing in jeopardy the promise of God to send the Messiah through the seed of the woman who would bruise the head of the serpent, the devil." And they rightly quote Mark 12 where it says in verse 25 that the angels in heaven are "neither married, nor given in marriage."

Hey, folks, whether these were mean demons or demonized men, the point the Bible is making is this: This was a world gone wild. People had totally turned their backs on God. In verse 3 of Genesis 6, God gives them a warning: "And the Lord said, 'My Spirit shall not strive with man forever.'"

I want to stop right here and express this: There are some of you who think God is going to keep giving you chance after chance to be saved, but He's not. He says that He's not going to strive with you forever. Jesus said in John 6:44, "No one can come to Me unless the Father who sent Me draws him." That's why 2 Corinthians 6:2 says, "Behold, now is the accepted time; behold, now is the day of salvation."

Some of you Christians are messing around with sin, and I'm telling you, God's about to blow your cover because His Spirit will not always strive with you. He's given you opportunity after opportunity to repent, and you haven't done it, and I'm telling you, judgment is coming. His Spirit will not always strive with you. There's a limit—not to what He can do in grace but to what He *will* do in grace. God is a holy God, and He will not put up with sin. Here's what Genesis 6:5-7 says:

> *Then the Lord saw that the wickedness of man was great in the earth, and that every intent of the thoughts of his heart was only evil continually. [Not just their actions but their attitudes. Not just their initiatives but their imaginations. Not just their works but their thoughts.] And the* Lord *was sorry that He had made man on the earth, and He was grieved in His heart. So, the* Lord *said, "I will destroy man whom I have created from the face of the earth, both man and beast, creeping thing and birds of the air, for I am sorry that I have made them."*

During Noah's lifetime, the world had become so wicked God said the only thing He could do with it was kill it. There were one or two other times when God sent destruction upon a city, like Sodom and Gomorrah, but evidently, this entire world was so sinful, the entire world had become so wicked and so corrupt, and mankind had become so evil that God said the only thing that could cleanse this world was a holy bath from heaven. He had to kill everything having breath in its nostrils and destroy every living thing on this earth! God had had enough, and God said enough was enough. He chose to wipe it all out and start over again.

"But Noah found grace in the eyes of the Lord" (Genesis 6:8). That's the first time grace is mentioned in the Bible. Here's a man in the middle of a wicked world, but just as God had said, there would be no half-way measures in executing judgment; there were no half-way measures in His effecting salvation. It was all of grace. Noah found grace in the eyes of the Lord. It's the grace Paul wrote about in Romans 5:20: "Where sin abounded, grace abounded much more."

The only way anyone can be saved from the judgment of God and the wrath of God is through the grace of God. Ephesians 2:8-9 says, "For by grace you have been saved through faith, and that not of yourselves; it is the gift of God, not of works, lest anyone should boast."

Noah was a sinner, just like all the others. He wasn't saved by his righteousness; he was saved by God's grace. Left to his own way and his own works, Noah would have drowned and died just like all the rest, but like Enoch, Noah responded to the Word of God and received the grace of God. As a result, he, like Enoch, "walked with God."

That ought to be a great encouragement to you today—to know that no matter how wicked the world may be, no matter how sinful society may become, because of God's grace, we can walk with the Lord in a wicked world.

WHEN GOD SPEAKS, OBEY IMMEDIATELY AND COMPLETELY

Do you have children? Do you like it when your children obey you? Well, can I tell you something? God likes it when His children obey Him, too. To me, this is one of the greatest things about Noah. If you're still there in Genesis, look down through chapter 6, and you'll find where God tells Noah that he's going to destroy the world. It literally says that He's going to "cut them off." So Noah wasn't just energized by God; he was enlightened by God. God told Noah that He was going to send a flood and destroy everybody and everything on the earth, but He was going to provide a way of escape through an ark that Noah would build. What a wonderful picture of salvation.

God gave Noah the instructions on how to build this boat, and we'll go through that in just a minute, but here's what I want you to see. In Genesis 6:22 it says, "Thus Noah did." He didn't debate it. He didn't discuss it. He didn't try to deny it. He simply did it. But here's the thing. It had never rained. Hebrews 11:7 says, "By faith Noah, being divinely warned of things not yet seen. . . ." God told Noah that He was going to destroy the entire world with a flood, but it had never even rained.

Up to this point, the Bible says in Genesis 2:5, "the Lord God had not caused it to rain on the earth . . . but a mist went up from the earth and watered the whole face of the ground." Bible scholars tell us that it had never rained before, and most likely, there was a water canopy that surrounded the earth, kind of like a bubble, and it created a hothouse effect that protected and preserved the world and everybody in it. That's one of the reasons why people lived so long in those days.

Noah had never seen it rain. He had never felt a drop of rain. But because God said it, Noah believed it and spent the next hundred years building that ark. He obeyed God immediately.

Can't you just see Noah? He's been working on that boat for ninety-nine years. God told him it was going to rain. The people would walk past the place where Noah was preparing that ark, and they would laugh at him and point at him and say, "Hey, Noah, what did you say your God told you it was going to do again?"

"It's going to rain."

"What's rain?"

"Rain is little drops of water that fall from the sky."

"It's never done anything like that before. What makes you think it's going to do it now?"

"God told me."

"God told you? Aw, you are crazy! You've been preaching that same sermon my entire life, and it hasn't rained yet."

"Well, God said it will rain and that He will destroy the world with water. You'd better get ready, and you'd better get right. It's going to rain."

Noah prepared for the flood for over one hundred years and preached that judgment was coming. That's why 2 Peter 2:5 calls Noah "a preacher of righteousness."

NOAH: A WORKING FAITH

He also obeyed God completely. Genesis 6:22 says, "Thus Noah did; according to all that God commanded him, so he did." Well, what did he do? He built that boat just like God told him: one hundred and fifty yards long, twenty-five yards wide, and fifteen yards high. It had three decks and many rooms, with one door made of cypress wood. The boat was completely sealed with pitch. It was a Westin Inn on water. It was a maritime Marriot. It was a holy Holiday Inn. Noah built that ark exactly like God had told him to.

Why is that so important? I'll tell you why. That ark is a picture of Jesus. It's a picture of salvation. You see, not only was salvation preached and proclaimed. It was pictured. How? Cypress wood is one of the hardest, most dense woods in the world, and it is a picture of the incorruptibility of the Lord Jesus. It had three floors, showing us that He was body, soul, and spirit. It was completely sealed with pitch, which is the same word for *atonement* in the Old Testament. And there was only one door—only one way into that ark of salvation.

What if Noah had said to God, "You know, I can find pine wood a lot easier than cypress wood. And, by the way, it's not as hard, so it won't wear out my saw. It won't be as hard to work with." What if Noah had said, "I don't like having to deal with that pitch stuff. It's too sticky. It's too smelly. I think I'll come up with something better"? What if Noah decided that he wanted to put another door on the other side because he thought it would look better or be easier to get the animals in? I mean, surely two doors are better than one. What if Noah had done all of that? I'll tell you what would have happened—he'd have drowned.

Listen when God tells you to do something, don't try to come up with your own plan. Don't try to do it your way. Don't customize God's commandment. When God speaks to you, just obey Him immediately and completely.

MAKE SURE YOUR FAMILY IS ON BOARD

Look back at Hebrews 11:7: "By faith Noah, being divinely warned of things not yet seen, moved with godly fear [he was mindful of the word of God, and as a result, he was moved by the fear of God so that he] prepared an ark for the saving of his household."

In Genesis 6:18, God said, "But I will establish My covenant with you; and you shall go into the ark; you, your sons, your wife, and your sons' wives with you." In 2 Peter 2:5, the Bible tells us how many people were on that boat: "But saved Noah, one of eight people, a preacher of righteousness, bringing in the flood on the world of the ungodly."

Noah preached for over one hundred years, and only seven people were saved, but he was a tremendous success. Why? Because he got his family on board. Let me tell you something: whatever else you do, make sure you and your family are on board. Make sure those little boys, girls, teenagers, and even your grown children know Jesus, love Jesus, and walk with Jesus.

Noah's grandfather, Enoch, walked with God, and Noah undoubtedly watched and learned how to walk with God by watching Enoch. Just like Enoch and Noah, you make sure your family learns to walk with God by watching and walking after you.

Why was it so important that Noah get all his sons and daughters-in-law on board that ark? Genesis 9:18-19 tells us why: "Now the sons of Noah who went out of the ark were Shem, Ham, and Japheth. And Ham was the father of Canaan. These three were the sons of Noah, and from these the whole earth was populated."

God killed everybody except Noah and his family, and He repopulated the entire world through those three sons. As a result, every single one of us can trace our family cypress tree back to the waterlogged section of Noah and his three boys. That's why it's so important that you make sure your family is on board.

I'll tell you, I've determined that I won't be like Billy Sunday, one of the greatest evangelists of another generation, who said his biggest heartbreak was that he's led countless souls to saving faith, but his own sons did not choose Christ.[9] Whatever else you do, Dad; whatever else you do, Mom, make sure your family is on board.

ACTIONS SPEAK LOUDER THAN WORDS

Look at Hebrews 11:7 one more time: "By which he condemned the world and became heir of the righteousness which is according to faith." What do we remember Noah for his preaching or his building? He's remembered for building that ark. But wait a minute. The Bible says that he was a preacher of righteousness. So, which speaks louder and longer, your words or your works? Your works. That's why James said in chapter 2, verse 18, "You have faith, and I have works. Show me your faith without your works, and I will show you my faith by my works."

I cannot work my soul to save, for that my Lord has done.[10]

---

9. Billy Sunday, original source unknown. Can be found in Edward K. Rowell, *1001 Quotes, Illustrations, and Humorous Stories for Preachers, Teachers, and Writers* (Grand Rapids, MI: Baker Books, 1996), 68.

10. Source unknown.

CHAPTER FOUR

ABRAHAM: AN OBEYING FAITH

Hebrews 11:8-10 and 17-19; Genesis 22:2

Hebrews 11 is the foundational chapter on faith in the Bible. In this chapter, the Holy Spirit defines, describes, and demonstrates what real faith is. In verse 1, we are given the definition of faith: "Now faith is the substance of things hoped for, the evidence of things not seen." Then, in verses 2 and 3, we are given the description of faith: "For by it [What? *Faith.*] the elders obtained a good testimony. By faith, we understand that the worlds were framed by the word of God, so the things which are seen were not made of visible things." As you continue reading, you find example after example, demonstration after demonstration, of faith exercised and exhibited in the lives of people just like you and me.

You know, often we read about people like Moses and Abraham and Isaac and Jacob and Sara and Rahab, and we get the idea they were some kind of super saints. We think of them as being so far ahead of us in their walks with the Lord that we could never have the kind of faith or be as faithful as they were. Well, just as a way of encouragement, let me give you something I've discovered that you may never have realized before: I believe one of the reasons why these particular people were placed in this portion of Scripture is because no matter whether you're young or old, male or female, rich or poor, there is somebody here you are going to be able to identify with. This really is a cross-section of society.

Here, we find young and old, rich and poor, male and female, educated and uneducated. So, no matter who you are, what you are, where you're from, or what your position may be, there is someone here who has walked where you're walking, has faced what you're facing, and was still able to exhibit and exercise great faith. That ought to be a great encouragement to you.

As we come to Hebrews 11:8, we are introduced to the most faithful man in all the Bible. (As a matter of fact, Romans 4 refers to him as "the father of the faith.") His name was Abraham, and here is what the Bible has to say about his amazing faith:

> *By faith Abraham obeyed when he was called to go out to the place which he would receive as an inheritance. And he went out, not knowing where he was going. By faith he dwelt in the land of promise as in a foreign country, dwelling in tents with Isaac and Jacob, the heirs with him of the same promise; for he waited for the city which has foundations, whose builder and maker is God. . . , By faith Abraham, when he was tested, offered up Isaac, and he who had received the promises offered up his only begotten son, of whom it was said, "In Isaac your seed shall be called," concluding that God was able to raise him up, even from the dead, from which he also received him in a figurative sense. (Hebrews 11:8-10, 17-19)*

ABRAHAM: AN OBEYING FAITH

Here is Abraham: The pivotal character in all the Old Testament; the acclaimed father of the world's three largest religions—Christianity, Judaism, and Islam; the one the Bible refers to at least three different times as "the friend of God." He is the most famous man of faith in all of history. He is the best known out of any of these giants of the faith mentioned in Hebrews 11. More verses are given to describe and demonstrate his faith than any other individual in the Bible.

So that raises the $24,000 question: what kind of faith did Abraham have?

The writer of Hebrews tells us: "By faith Abraham obeyed" (11:8). The kind of faith that Abraham demonstrated and displayed was obeying faith. It was the characteristic of his life. I believe it's what made him "a friend of God." He had an obeying faith.

Obedience was such a significant characteristic of his life that Warren Wiersbe's book on Abraham's life is even entitled *Be Obedient: Learning the Secret of Living by Faith*. Or, as the old hymn we sang growing up says, "Trust and obey, for there's no other way to be happy in Jesus than to trust and obey."

It has been well said that "every great person first learned how to obey, whom to obey, and when to obey." If that's true, and I believe that it is, then Abraham was truly great. He learned how to obey—completely. He learned whom to obey—God. And he learned when to obey—now.

Let's examine Abraham's life and learn this simple secret of living by faith: obedience. Hebrews 11 teaches four major principles through Abraham's faith. Here's the first one.

SIMPLE OBEDIENCE LEADS TO POWERFUL BLESSINGS

Look at verse 8 again. See what the writer of Hebrews says: "By faith, Abraham obeyed when he was called to go out to the place which he would receive as an inheritance." To understand the significance of that statement, you've got to go all the way back to the dark days of Abraham's life before he met God. If you were to turn back to Genesis chapter 11, you would begin to read about this man who would become the father of the faithful, but at this point in his life, he isn't full of faith at all. He's a pagan living in "Ur of the Chaldeans."

Now, I need to tell you a little bit about Ur of the Chaldeans before we go much further because you need to understand where Abraham was and what he was to comprehend the significance of his obedience fully. Ur of the Chaldeans wasn't just a wide spot in the desert; it was a great city. It was a center of civilization—a seat of worldly prosperity. As a matter of fact, back in the 1920s and 30s, Sir Leonard Woolley, the great archaeologist, excavated this ancient city, and he discovered high walls and harbors; big, beautiful buildings; houses and streets laid out in blocks; and evidence of great wealth and education. It was a wealthy city, and it was worldly, but it was also a wicked city because the biggest and most elaborate building that Woolley discovered was a Ziggurat, a temple built for the moon god "Nanna," and a mass grave that gives evidence of human sacrifice.

R. Kent Hughes writes in his commentary on Genesis, "These treasures of Ur tell us that Abraham's social and religious context was as sophisticated and pagan and claustrophobic as that of any Babylonian or Egyptian dynasty. Ur was desolate and barren of knowledge of the true God. Ur's intrusive lunar religion dominated life from birth to the grave."[11]

So here's Abraham, living in a wealthy but wicked city. He's already done very well for himself. He was a successful businessman. He was married to a beautiful woman. Everybody who worked for him admired him and respected him. He had

---

11. Taken from *Genesis: Beginning and Blessing* by Kent R. Hughes, © 2012, p. 182. Used by permission of Crossway, a publishing ministry of Good News Publishers, Wheaton, IL 60187, www.crossway.org.

ABRAHAM: AN OBEYING FAITH

the right pedigree to go somewhere and become somebody because he could trace his family tree back to Adam. But as rich as he was, as respected as he was, as religious as he was when the story of Abraham opens, he's nothing more than a poor, lost sinner rushing into a lost eternity.

You see, just like every single saved person, there was a time in Abraham's life when he did not know the One true God. As a matter of fact, there was a time when Abraham wasn't even Abraham; he was simply known as "Abram." (He was just half the man we know and admire today.) But in that devilish darkness, he saw the light of the world. In all the hustle and bustle of that wicked city, he heard the bare word of God, and he believed the bare word of God, and he simply obeyed the bare word of God.

Look at Genesis 12:1, 4: "Now the Lord had said to Abram: "Get out of your country, from your family and from your father's house to a land that I will show you.". . . So Abram departed as the Lord had spoken to him."

God talked, and Abraham walked. There was a revelation, and then there was a response. There was a statement of faith, and then there was a step of faith. Abraham heard the voice of God, and he heeded it. He simply and immediately obeyed God.

At Fort Bragg, North Carolina, a clerical error sent a supply clerk with the 82nd Airborne out the door of an airplane without any formal training. When asked why he jumped, he said that he was just following orders. "The army said that I was qualified, and I wasn't going to question it."

What happened? Abraham was saved by God. He was saved by grace through faith. He no longer worshipped the moon god; now, he worshipped the One who created the moon. He no longer tried to store up treasures in this world; he began to store up treasures in heaven. He no longer lived for this world; he looked for the world to come. He was saved by grace through faith.

Then, he was set apart by God. Look in the middle of verse 1 in Genesis 12: "Get out of your country, from your family and from your father's house, to a land that I will show you. I will make you a great nation; I will bless you and make your name great; and you shall be a blessing. I will bless those who bless you, and I will curse him who curses you; and in you all the families of the earth shall be blessed" (vv. 1-3).

Five times in three verses, God says, "I will," "I will," "I will," "I will," "I will." It was all of God, and it was all of grace.

What you have here is one of, if not the most important, passages in all the Old Testament. This is what is known as the "Abrahamic Covenant." It's a powerful blessing, a personal promise that God made with Abraham because of his simple obedience.

So here is the principle we learn from Abraham: Simple obedience leads to powerful blessing. Abraham already had a lot, but God wanted to give him more. Abraham already had a good name, but God wanted to give him a great name. The name "Abram" meant "exalted father." Moreover, because of his obedient faith, God made him "Abraham"— "father of a multitude."

Do you want the blessings of God? Then trust God and obey God. Trust him with your family like Abraham did. Trust him with your finances like Abraham did. Trust him with your fame and your future like Abraham did because simple obedience brings powerful blessings.

THE WAY FORWARD IS BY LOOKING UPWARD

Go back to Hebrews chapter 11 for just a moment. There's something the writer of Hebrews spells out for us that Moses didn't do back in Genesis chapter 12. Hebrews 11:8 says, "By faith, Abraham obeyed when he was called to go out to

ABRAHAM: AN OBEYING FAITH

the place which he would receive as an inheritance. [Now, we know all of that, but pay attention to how the writer of Hebrews describes his response.] And he went out, not knowing where he was going."

Like I told you in the previous chapter, delayed obedience isn't obedience at all. This was literally a step of faith because when God called Abraham to leave Ur, He didn't spread a map of the Fertile Crescent, the Middle East, out on the floor and say, "All right, here we are, and over here's where we're going. I'm going to take you here, and you're going to camp here, and then you're going to go through here." That's not what the Lord did at all. He didn't take him up in the clouds and show him the path that he was going to take to this Promised Land.

Again, that's not what God did at all. He didn't show Abraham the whole journey; He just told Abraham to take the first step, and the rest of the steps would be revealed as he and God walked together.

You know, that's exactly the way it is in our Christian walk. That's what it means to "walk by faith and not by sight." Sure, there are those wonderful times when the path is marked, and the Lord tells us where we're going and how we're going to get there, but that doesn't happen very often. Most of the time, the Lord gives us just enough light to see the next step in front of us—and sometimes not even that much. We just have to walk by faith, trusting that our great Guide knows the way.

One morning, I had to get up early and go outside to get a bag for my wife, Kim, out of the truck. As I was rubbing my eyes and trying to stay awake, I looked up, and wow, the sky was clear. I could see many stars sparkling and shining. But there was one star shining brighter than any of the others. It was the North Star.

Back before compasses or GPS units, travelers and sailors navigated using the North Star. They knew that one star was always north, so they could always use the constant position of that star to help them figure out which way to go.

Hey, in the fast-changing world in which we live today, there is one constant—One who never changes, One whose position is fixed. He's called the "Bright and Morning Star" (Revelation 22:16). His name is Jesus, and you can set your course, and you can fix your life, and you can walk through this world if you will just look up and keep your eyes on Him. That's why the writer of Hebrews wrote, "Looking unto Him, the author and finisher of our faith" (Hebrews 12:2).

DON'T LIVE FOR EARTHLY THINGS; LOOK FOR ETERNAL THINGS

Study verses 9-10 in Hebrews chapter 11: "By faith he dwelt in the land of promise as in a foreign country, dwelling in tents with Isaac and Jacob, the heirs with him of the same promise; for he waited for the city which has foundations, whose builder and maker is God."

The word *looked* literally means "earnestly expected." Abraham was longing and looking for more than he saw in Ur or even Canaan. He understood that even the majestic buildings of Ur would eventually crumble into dust. He knew the things of this world won't and can't last, so he was laying up for himself "treasures in heaven, where neither moth nor rust destroys and where thieves do not break in and steal [Why? Because he knew that—]. . . . where your treasure is, there your heart will be also" (Matthew 6:20).

I watch so many people today, and the way they live and the way they work gives me the impression that they either think they're going to live forever or that they'll get to take it all with them when they die. Listen, nobody will live forever. First, Peter 1:24 says that "all flesh is like grass." It's green one day and gone the next. I've done a lot of funerals, but I've never seen a U-Haul trailer behind a hearse. You can't take it with you when you die.

Do you want to know why Abraham was looking and longing and living for that city? I'll tell you why: he was eternally invested. God's call was so clear, and His vision was so vivid that Abraham didn't want to get too attached to the things down here. Heaven was where his heart was—so much so that he didn't fit in with the folks down here.

I know this doesn't make sense to some of you. The world says, "Settle down, be safe, make a name for yourself." We naturally want to be more comfortable. We naturally want huge homes, power, and prestige, but God's Word instructs us to do the exact opposite. Colossians 3:1-3 says, "Seek those things which are above, where Christ is, sitting at the right hand of God. Set your mind on things above, not on things on the earth. For you died, and your life is hidden with Christ in God."

IN ORDER TO RECEIVE ALL THAT GOD HAS, YOU'VE GOT TO GIVE ALL THAT YOU HAVE

In Hebrews 11:17-19, we are told about the supreme test of faith and the supreme act of obedience in all of the Old Testament. The Bible says, "By faith Abraham, when he was tested, offered up Isaac, and he who had received the promises offered up his only begotten son, of whom it was said, 'In Isaac your seed shall be called,' concluding that God was able to raise him up, even from the dead, from which he also received him in a figurative sense."

Do you want to know what makes Abraham the "father of the faithful"? You just read it. You see, Abraham wasn't just a giant of the faith because he was willing to go somewhere that he had never been before. Abraham is a giant of the faith because he was willing to give up everything he ever had and everything he ever would have because God told him to.

God said, "Take now your son, your only son Isaac, whom you love, and go to the land of Moriah, and offer him there as a burnt offering on one of the mountains of which I shall tell you" (Genesis 22:2).

God came to Abraham again, and He said, "Abraham."

"Yes, Lord."

"I want you to take Isaac, the son of your Old age, your only begotten son, the son that I promised you would become a great nation as numerous as the sands on the seashore, and I want you to take him to a place that I'm going to show you, and I want you to kill him and burn him as an offering to me."

And Abraham obeyed God.

It's been said that Abraham believed God and obeyed God when he didn't know where, when he didn't know when, when he didn't know how, and when he didn't know why. That's a man of great faith. And you know the story: Abraham and Isaac climbed up that mountain, and Abraham placed Isaac on that altar and was just about to thrust that knife into the chest of his only son—that son of the promise—when he heard the Angel of the Lord (which, by the way, I believe is Jesus) tell him to stop and kill the ram caught by its horns in the thicket behind him instead. What a wonderful picture of what Jesus did for us on the cross. As a matter of fact, Jesus even said in John 8:56, "Your father Abraham rejoiced to see my day, and he saw it and was glad."

You say, "Well, that's not really faith. He knew that God wasn't going to let him kill Isaac." That's not what the Bible says! The Bible says in Hebrews 11 that he trusted God so much that if he killed Isaac because God told him to, then God would raise Isaac up—He would resurrect him to keep the promise He had made with Abraham. Now, that is great faith!

Abraham believed God so much that, in his mind, he had already offered Isaac up as a dead sacrifice, but God gave him back to Abraham as a living sacrifice. He had to give all to receive all.

Do you know why that's true? First Samuel 15:22 tells us, "To obey is better than sacrifice, and to heed than the fat of rams." Oswald Chambers wrote, "The best measure of a spiritual life is not its ecstasies, but its obedience."[12]

The Lord is looking for surrender and complete sacrifice.

---

12. Oswald Chambers, *Not Knowing Whither: The Steps of Abraham's Faith*, 2nd ed. (Grand Rapids, MI: Our Daily Bread Publishing, 2021). Used with permission.

CHAPTER FIVE

SARAH: A RECEIVING FAITH

Hebrews 11:11-12; Genesis 18:11-15

Hebrews chapter 11 really is an amazing chapter. (I know that I have said that in every chapter, but it's still true.) As a matter of fact, it's one of the greatest chapters in the entire Bible.

It's right up there with John chapter 3 and Romans chapter 8. I think the reason is because whereas John chapter 3 tells how we're loved, and Romans chapter 8 tells us how we're liberated, Hebrews chapter 11 tells us how to live. And it does it in a way that connects with just about every one of us.

What the writer of Hebrews (who I think was Paul, but no one is certain) does is this: he gives us, in this chapter, little snapshots of people who lived for God and loved God, just like we want to do today. A snapshot is a simple picture. It's not meant to detail every single aspect of the person. It's not meant to communicate their whole life story. It simply gives you the essence of the person.

But here's the great thing about these pictures, these snapshots—especially for the men and women mentioned in this great chapter: they only show their good side. I heard about a woman who went to one of these fancy-schmancy, glamour-type photography studios to have her picture taken. After the session, she went back to review the portrait the photographer had picked out, and she didn't like it at all. She ranted and raged. She fussed, and she fumed. She looked at that photographer and said, "That's not even what I look like. I'm much prettier in person than I am in that photo. It doesn't capture my good side. It doesn't do me justice." And the photographer looked back at her and said, "Lady, you don't need justice; you need mercy."

That's kind of what the writer of Hebrews did for these folks: he captured their good side. Or maybe, to put it better, he captured their "godly side." He took a snapshot of them when they were at their best for God.

Here in this chapter, they don't have the sleep of sin in their eyes. Their hair isn't messed up from running from God. They have on their Sunday morning clothes, not their Friday night clothes. They're made up on the outside as well as the inside. And at just the right moment, at just the right angle, with all the proper lighting, their picture is taken and placed up on the mantle of Scripture for you and me to learn from and live by today.

I don't know if you know this or not, but four times in the Bible, God tells us that "the just shall live by faith." Now, how do you do that? How do you live by faith? I mean, it's easy to say it, but doing it is a different issue altogether. I'll tell you how: by looking at and learning from these powerful pictures—these spiritual snapshots—of the heroes of the faith listed for us in Hebrews chapter 11.

As the old saying goes, "Seeing is believing." Or, like somebody reminded me this past week, "Faith isn't just taught; it's caught." That's my prayer as we study these mighty men and wonderful women of the faith. Yes, I pray that you'll learn the tremendous truths we're taught through this text. But even more than learning about worship, I pray you'll begin to worship. Even more than learning how to walk with God, I pray you'll begin to walk with God. Even more than learning about obedience, I pray you'll begin to simply and immediately obey God.

In the last chapter, we learned about the obeying faith of Abraham. We saw the Bible refer to him as "the father of all those who believe." Well, if Abraham is "the father of the faith," then the lovely lady we are introduced to in verse 11 must be "the mother of the faith" because she's Abraham's wife and Isaac's mother.

In Hebrews 11:11, we are told that "by faith Sarah herself also received strength to conceive seed, and she bore a child when she was past the age, because she judged Him faithful who had promised." Here, we are given the spiritual snapshot of Sarah's remarkable, receiving faith. Sarah received her name from the Lord when He said in Genesis 17:15, "As for Sarai your wife, you shall not call her name Sarai, but Sarah shall be her name."

The name Sarah means "queen." This explains why God went on to say in the next verse, "She shall be a mother of nations; kings of peoples shall be from her" (Genesis 17:16). That's why, in his book entitled *All the Women of the Bible*, Herbert Lockyer wrote that Sarah was "one of the most important female figures in the world's history [because she was], the natural source of the Jewish people, through whom the nations of the earth were to be blessed."[13]

Sarah's one of only two women mentioned by name in God's great hall of great faith. She was the first, and Rahab was the second, and they both lived by faith and died by faith. She was such a beautiful lady that men were still fighting over her when she was in her eighties. She was a gorgeous geriatric. As one writer put it, "Sarah seemed to have had a beauty that

---

13. Taken from *All the Women of the Bible* by Herbert Lockyer. Copyright © 1967 by Herbert Lockyer. Used by permission of HarperCollins Christian Publishing. www.harpercollinschristian.com.

grew more attractive with the passing years." And ladies, if all that wasn't enough to make you dislike her, she was even able to travel well. How many of you look your best after spending days in a car traveling on your family vacation? How many of you would be willing to enter the Miss America Pageant after traveling cross-country with a carload of kids and no functioning air-conditioning?

Well, Sarah traveled through the dusty deserts of Egypt under a scorching sun for months and was more beautiful when she arrived than when she left. As a matter of fact, it kind of caught Abraham off guard because he said, "You're so beautiful; we've got to tell everybody that you're my sister and not my wife, or they'll kill me just to get you."

So she was beautiful, and she was blessed, but here's the problem: she was also barren. She was unable to have children, and that's the whole point of Hebrews 11:11. God had told her that she was going to conceive and give birth to a son through whom the whole world would be blessed, but there was another problem. She was past her childbearing years. She was past the time when women can conceive and give birth to a child. The Bible says that she'd even gone through menopause, but despite all of that, she believed and conceived and received the son that God had promised.

Now, that's the simple point the snapshot of Hebrews 11:11 gives to us. If you were to just take a quick glance at what the Bible says, that's what you'd see. But there's so much more here than you'd catch in a passing glance. So, on these pages, I want to show you what we learn from the remarkable receiving faith of this lovely lady named Sarah.

A PERSONAL FAITH IS A POWERFUL FAITH

Looking still at Hebrews 11:11, Sarah's faith is described in this way: "By faith Sarah herself also...." In other words, we're talking about Sarah's *faith* specifically. We're not talking about Abraham's faith at this point. This was Sarah's personal faith. She wasn't riding on Abraham's coattails; she wasn't depending on his faith. She had a personal faith all her own. That's what gave her the personal power we have described for us here in verse 11.

I want you to think about how powerful Sarah's personal faith was. Her faith enabled her to leave the only home she'd ever known to wander those dry, dusty deserts and live in tents. It enabled her to give up all the creature comforts ladies love and to rough it for the rest of her life. It enabled her to follow this free-spirited man she'd fallen in love with all over that part of the world when he didn't even know where he was going. (Of course, Abraham never asked for directions, either. Sound familiar, ladies?) Her faith enabled her to conceive a child when she was too old to do so naturally, and then it enabled her to watch her husband walk off toward a mountain to kill that child because that's what God told him to do. You can't do all of that on borrowed faith.

Faith, by its very nature, must be personal, or it really isn't faith at all. You can't even spell the word without using the letter "I." In 1 Peter chapter 1, Peter reminds us, "You won't make it to heaven on your father's faith." But the sad fact is there are many people today who are doing just that. They're betting their eternity on a borrowed faith. And I'll tell you, a borrowed faith isn't worth half of a hallelujah to get you to heaven.

If you think you're going to heaven because your father or your mother or your brother or your sister or your best friend has placed their faith in God, you're in for a really rude awakening. There is a commonly known phrase, "God doesn't have grandchildren." The only faith powerful enough to get you to heaven is personal faith.

Not only will you not make it to heaven on a borrowed faith, but you also won't make it through this world on a borrowed faith. Think back to Sarah. She was a lady like many of you. She faced the same kinds of hurts and heartaches you face. She faced sickness and suffering just like you've faced. She was fearful of the unknown. She was not able to have a child, which was seen as a mark of God's divine disfavor, and it broke her heart. She and Abraham had their fusses and their fights, those times when you could hear them at the other end of the camp when Abraham gave her an ultimatum, and she slammed the door of the tent and went to sleep somewhere else. She had her heart ripped out when she learned of Abraham's affair with Hagar. And, what about later, when she thought she was going to lose her only child because her husband said he'd heard the voice of God?

Did Sarah face the same kind of things that we face today? Sure, she did. Well then, how did she make it through all those trials and temptations? I'll tell you this. It wasn't on a rented, second-hand, hand-me-down, borrowed kind of faith.

No! Sarah simply received and remembered the truth you and I read about in 1 Corinthians 10:13, where it says, "No temptation [that means no test, no trial, no tough time] has overtaken you except such as is common to man; but God is faithful . . . so that you may be able to bear it."

How can you make it through this world? By exercising your personal faith in the Person and purpose of Jesus every day, because, as that faith is exercised, it won't just be personal—it will become powerful.

OUR PROBLEMS ARE GOD'S OPPORTUNITIES

Hebrews 11:11 tells us about Sarah's problem. "By faith Sarah herself also received strength to conceive seed, and she bore a child when she was past the age." That's kind of like reading the end of a suspense novel to see how it's going to turn out before you start reading. How many of you do that? Well, Sarah had a problem. And her problem was that she was unable to have children. Yes, she was blessed, and yes, she was beautiful, but she was also barren.

Read what the Bible says in Genesis 11:29-30: "Then Abram and Nahor took wives: the name of Abram's wife was

SARAH: A RECEIVING FAITH

Sarai, and the name of Nahor's wife, Milcah, the daughter of Haran the father of Milcah and the father of Iscah. [Here's the problem:] But Sarai was barren; she had no child." You see, back in Sarah's day, back in Sarah's time, barrenness was one of the worst things in the world that could happen to a woman. Children—especially male children—were very important to these people. They were important to carry on the family name. They were intended to carry on the family's religion. And so the ability to have children—a lot of children—was seen as a sign of God's blessings.

I know that sounds archaic and out of date for us today because today, children are often referred to as a burden or a bother instead of a blessing. But I want to remind you the Bible still says, "Children are a heritage from the Lord, the fruit of the womb is a reward. Like arrows in the hand of a warrior, so are the children of one's youth" (Psalm 127:3-4).

Children are a gift from God. The Bible says here that Sarah's inability to have children was a real problem. (By the way, all three of the main mother figures of Israel—Sarah, Abraham's wife; Rebecca, Isaac's wife; and Rachel, Jacob's wife— had problems with barrenness, and yet in every one of them, God supernaturally opened their womb and gave them children.)

Sarah doesn't and seemingly can't have children. She's a barren woman, and she desperately wants to be able to give a son to her husband, Abraham, but now she's seventy-five years old, and it looks like all hope is gone.

Let me say this to you today: You may be here right now, and you feel like all hope is gone. You may think that you have a problem no one can fix. It's beyond hope. Listen. It's not beyond hope because nothing is too hard for God!

That's exactly what the Bible says in Genesis 18. Sarah had a real problem, but she received a promise. She wasn't really spiritual about it, though. As a matter of fact, some might have said she was sacrilegious, but God gave it to her anyway.

God had already told Abraham he was going to give him a son through Sarah, but Abraham faltered in his faith. He stumbled in his walk with God, so God came to Abraham again just to remind him, and He let Sarah listen. The Bible says in Genesis 18:10-15,

> *"Sarah your wife shall have a son." (Sarah was listening in the tent door which was behind him.) Now Abraham and Sarah were old, well advanced in age; and Sarah had passed the age of childbearing. Therefore, Sarah laughed within herself, saying, "After I have grown old, shall I have pleasure, my lord [that's Abraham] being old also?" And the LORD said to Abraham, "Why did Sarah laugh, saying, 'Shall I surely bear a child, since I am old?' Is anything too hard for the LORD? At the appointed time I will return to you, according to the time of life, and Sarah shall have a son." But Sarah denied it, saying, "I did not laugh," for she was afraid. And He said, "No, but you did laugh!"*

Let me share this with you because it's good. Sarah had a problem: barrenness. God gave her a promise: "You're going to have a boy." And just to remind her of her momentary unbelief when she laughed at the promise of God, God named that boy Isaac, which means "laughter."

Do you have a problem? Then listen to this pastor. If you've got a problem, you need to quit calling everybody. You need to quit complaining about how bad things are. You need to quit pouting and panicking about how you're going to get out of this hole you've gotten yourself into. You need to get alone with God, open your Bible, and start reading your Bible until a promise jumps off that page and burns into your heart. Then you take that promise and claim that promise and hold onto that promise no matter what. You see, a problem is nothing more than an opportunity for God to show His power because nothing is too hard for Him.

SARAH: A RECEIVING FAITH

MISTRUSTING GOD LEADS TO GREAT MISTAKES

This is huge. The very fact that Sarah, or Abraham, even made it into this listing of the faithful is evidence that God is a God of grace and forgiveness. It's evidence that, as the old country preachers used to say, "God can hit a big lick with a crooked stick." I mean, they blew it big time. Now, don't let that bother you. Don't let somebody else's shortcomings cause you to stumble. Donald Barnhouse, a great Presbyterian preacher, once said, "No perfect feet walk the path of faith."[14] We all have feet of clay, and we all stumble in our faith. The only difference between Abraham and Sarah and you and me at this point was that they did it on Primetime.

You say, "What in the world did they do?" They got ahead of God. They tried to help God out, and as a result, the world is still paying the price for their sin. Let me make a really long story short. Sarah got impatient waiting for God to give her a son to fulfill the promise He'd made to Abraham, so she gave her little slave girl, Hagar, to Abraham. Abraham slept with Hagar; she got pregnant and had a little boy named Ishmael (who God Himself said would be a "wild man"), and the world has never been the same.

Ishmael, just like God had said He would, became the leader of a great nation just like his half-brother Isaac. He fathered the Ishmaelites who fought Isaac's descendants—the children of Israel, the Jewish people—all throughout the Old Testament. From the Ishmaelites came the Arabs, and from the Arabs came a man named Mohammed, who had a series of perverted, demonic dreams that developed into the evil religion you and I know today as Islam. And so, all the heartache, bloodshed, and violence you and I see, read about, and experience today from

---

14. Donald Barnhouse, taken from *Genesis: Beginning and Blessing* by Kent R. Hughes, © 2012, p. 237. Used by permission of Crossway, a publishing ministry of Good News Publishers, Wheaton, IL 60187, www.crossway.org.

the followers of Mohammed can be traced back to a woman by the name of Sarah who thought she knew better than God. She tried to help God out and got the world into a whole lot of trouble. How many of you know that when you try to help God out, you end up messing everything up?

Here's the point. When you get ahead of God, you get an Ishmael—a "wild man." But when you wait on the Lord, when you trust in the Lord, you get an Isaac—"the son of the promise."

Never forget this truth.

It's not unusual for you to have to wait on the Lord. It's not unusual for God to be silent. (As a matter of fact, God's been silent far more than He's spoken.) John Phillips said, "His silences are as eloquent as His sayings."[15]

God speaks, and then He waits for faith to operate. The sad fact about this story is that instead of faith triumphing, the flesh triumphed. Mistrusting God led to a great mistake.

YOU CAN TRUST GOD'S HEART WHEN YOU CAN'T TRACE HIS HAND

Charles Haddon Spurgeon said that even if we don't see God's hand in our situation, we can always trust He knows what's best. And that's ultimately what Sarah did.[16] Oh. To be sure, she messed up just like we all do, but ultimately and finally and completely, she placed her trust in the promise of God, and God fulfilled that promise by the giving of that son, Isaac when she was ninety years old. That's why Hebrews 11:11 says, "Because she judged Him faithful who had promised."

---

15. Taken from *Exploring Genesis: An Expository Commentary*, p. 137 © Copyright 1980 by John Phillips. Published by Kregel Publications, Grand Rapids, MI. Used by permission of the publisher. All rights reserved.

16. Charles Haddon Spurgeon, in John C. Maxwell's *Wisdom from Women in the Bible: Giants of the Faith Speak Into Our Lives* (Nashville, TN: FaithWords, 2015).

One day, when you get a chance, you ought to sit down and begin digging through and discovering all the promises of the Word of God. Hebrews 13:5 tells us, "I will never leave you nor forsake you." Romans 8:28 says, "And we know that all things work together for good to those who love God, to those who are the called according to His purpose." John 6:37 promises, "All that the Father gives Me will come to Me, and the one who comes to Me I will by no means cast out." Jeremiah 31:34 tells us, "I will forgive their iniquity, and their sin I will remember no more." Philippians 4:13 says, "I can do all things through Christ who strengthens me." Second Corinthians 12:9 adds, "My grace is sufficient for you, for My strength is made perfect in weakness."

You read those promises, and you receive those promises, and even when you can't see God moving, when you can't hear God talking, when you don't understand what's going on or why, when things don't make sense, you can take God at His Word and you can trust the heart of God because, even when we aren't, God is faithful!

CHAPTER SIX

ISAAC: A FAMILY FAITH

Hebrews 11:20; Genesis 25–27

In Hebrews 11:20, we read, "By faith, Isaac blessed Jacob and Esau concerning things to come." Over the past five chapters, we've been walking and working our way down through the mighty men and wonderful women identified for us in *God's Hall of Faith*. Up to this point, we've worshipped with Abel, walked with Enoch, and worked with Noah. We've seen Abraham believe the promise of God, and we've seen Sarah receive the promise of God. We've watched these great men and women soar in the thrill of victory, but we've also watched them stumble in the agony of defeat. However, in all and through all, we've seen the expression and the exhibition of great faith in their lives. (This is why we're even studying them to begin with.)

In this chapter, we come to a man by the name of Isaac, and I must admit, it's been hard to get excited about the life of

Isaac. The reason for that is that very little is exciting about his life. He was the ordinary son of an extraordinary father and the ordinary father of an extraordinary son. There was nothing really extraordinary about him at all.

Looking at Abraham and Isaac side by side, there is an amazing contrast between them—so much so that you wouldn't even know they were father and son. Abraham was wild and wandering; Isaac was dull and domesticated. Abraham was a powerful figure; Isaac was very much a sensitive figure. Abraham was active; Isaac was passive. Abraham had the foreign mission; Isaac had the home mission. Abraham had to rule a world; Isaac had to raise a family. Abraham founded nations; Isaac dug wells. Abraham ran to his fights; Isaac ran from his fights. Abraham walked in the world and restrained evil; Isaac walked within his own house and restrained himself. Abraham guided nations; Isaac nurtured children.

After studying Isaac's life, the best thing I can say about his personality and character is that he devoted himself to hearth and home. He was a homebody in every way. He was a family man. That is why I have described his faith as a "family faith," because everything in and about Isaac's life is founded and focused on his family.

In that way, Isaac is an excellent example for us today. Here, we have a man who loved and lived for his family. He was a family man, and he was a faithful man. He was a good man, and in many ways, he was a godly man. The interesting thing about the life and testimony of Isaac is this: less is said about him than any of the other patriarchs. There is more description and detail given to Abraham's life and faith than his son Isaac's. There is more description and detail given to Jacob's life and faith than his father, Isaac. The Bible uses some twelve chapters to detail the lives of Abraham, Jacob, and Joseph, but except for a few brief statements before and after, the history of Isaac is condensed into just two chapters: Genesis 26 and 27.

ISAAC: A FAMILY FAITH

IT TAKES A FAITHFUL MAN TO BUILD A FAITHFUL FAMILY

Let me be clear: this is not to put down or diminish single mothers at all. It's just that there really is no way to completely or adequately replace a godly mother and a godly father working together in the raising and rearing of children. And since, according to the Bible, the husband is to be the head of the home and the priest for his family, there is an amazing amount of responsibility that falls on that father for the faith and faithfulness of his family.

About twenty or so years ago, Hillary Clinton wrote a book that received much attention and publicity entitled *It Takes a Village.* I understand her whole point in writing and publishing that book was to take the responsibility for raising children away from their parents and ultimately place it in the state's hands. Well, as I read the Bible, I don't find where it says it takes a village. What I find is where the Bible says that it takes a *family*. Furthermore, a family desperately needs a father's loving and spiritual leadership.

I want you to understand. Your family is going to be just as faithful to the Lord and the things of God as you are. You're going to be the thermostat that is going to determine the spiritual temperature of your home. "As the father goes, so goes the family."

As you study the life of Isaac, this is about the only place where he halfway shines. The one thing that you can say about Isaac is that he was faithful to his family. As a matter of fact, I don't know if you're aware of this, but Isaac is the only one of the patriarchs of the Jewish nation who only had one wife. As you read about Abraham, you'll find that he had numerous wives and concubines. As you read about Jacob, you'll find he had numerous wives and concubines. Joseph had more than one wife. Even David, a man after God's own heart, wasn't a one-woman man. And Solomon, the wisest man who ever lived, had over a thousand wives and concubines—which leads me to doubt just how smart he really was.

But as you study the Scripture, what you'll find is that Isaac was a one-woman man. He was a faithful, as well as faith-filled, husband. And gentlemen, we are given a glimpse of what it means to be the spiritual leader of our families in two tremendous prayers that he prayed. In the first prayer, he prayed for a wife. And in the second prayer, he prayed for a child.

The first prayer is found in Genesis 24:63-67 where the Bible tells us about Abraham's servant returning with Rebekah, who will become Isaac's wife:

> *And Isaac went out to meditate [that word literally means "to walk and pray"] in the field in the evening; and he lifted his eyes and looked, and there, the camels were coming. Then Rebekah lifted her eyes, and when she saw Isaac she dismounted from her camel; for she had said to the servant, "Who is this man walking in the field to meet us?" The servant said, "It is my master." So she took a veil and covered herself. And the servant told Isaac all the things that he had done. Then Isaac brought her into his mother Sarah's tent; and he took Rebekah and she became his wife, and he loved her. So Isaac was comforted after his mother's death.*

Here was a man, forty years old, who had lost his mother, and the Bible says her death grieved him. It hurt him. And so, he was out walking and talking to God, no doubt about his hopes and his hurts and his desire for a wife, when right at that moment, the woman who would become his wife came riding over the hill on a camel. (Praise God for a woman who can ride a camel, amen?) The Bible says that he took her into his mother's tent, and she became his wife, and he loved her.

I'll tell you, there's a word there for those of you who aren't married but one day hope to be. Instead of talking to your friends and your family about helping you find a husband or a wife, talk to God. Instead of getting on the internet and talking in some chat room to somebody, get out and walk and talk with God. Instead of going to the clubs and looking for some bar stool buzzard, go to the fields and let God lead you to that one to whom you can give your heart. Just walk and talk with God.

There's also a word here for those of you who are married—and especially the men. If you want to have a lovely marriage, love your mate. The Bible says it explicitly: "And he loved her" (Genesis 24:67). That means that he didn't just say he loved her; he showed that he loved her. He spent more time at home than he did at the office. He cared more about spending time with her than he cared about spending time with the boys. He wasn't out looking for somebody else; he had all that he ever wanted or needed at home.

I'll tell you something, guys: the best thing that you could do for your marriage is to stay close to home. Instead of thinking that somebody you work with or run into is "hot," you make sure that you keep the fire burning at home. I've seen it hundreds of times—a wandering eye will lead you down a crooked path that will ultimately destroy your home, your reputation, and your walk with God. If you're not faithful to your wife, you really aren't faithful at all. (There's a reason God compares turning your back on Him to adultery.)

Isaac loved Rebekah. He prayed for the woman of his dreams, and God gave him the desires of his heart.

There's another prayer Isaac prayed as well. Not only did he pray for a wife, but he prayed for a child. If you look in verse 19 of Genesis chapter 25, you'll see where the Bible begins to give the genealogy of Isaac. It says in verses 19- 21, 26, "This is the genealogy of Isaac, Abraham's son. Abraham begot Isaac. Isaac was forty years old when he took Rebekah as his wife, the daughter of Bethuel the Syrian of Padan Aram, the sister of Laban the Syrian. Now Isaac pleaded with the Lord for his wife, because she was barren; and the Lord granted his plea, and Rebekah his wife conceived. . . . Isaac was sixty years old when she bore them."

Rebekah was barren, just like Isaac's mother, Sarah, had been. But Isaac was the son of promise. Through him was promised a mighty nation that would be a blessing to the whole world. But they had been married for a little while and still had no children. Evidently, it started to bother Rebekah more than it did him, and so the Bible says that Isaac began to plead with the Lord for his wife, and the Lord granted his plea. Rebekah, his wife, conceived.

Now, that's a great miracle displaying the faithfulness of God. But I don't want you to miss the faithfulness of this future father. How old does the Bible say Isaac was when he and Rebekah got married? He was forty years old. How old was he when she had those twin boys? He was sixty. So, for somewhere around twenty years, Isaac prayed and pleaded and petitioned God to give his wife a child, and the Lord didn't just answer his prayer—He gave them a double portion. She gave birth to twins. That's the power of a praying husband!

Like the old bumper sticker says, "The family that prays together stays together." Perhaps the greatest example of a faithful family that I've ever been around wasn't even my family. It was a family that I lived with for a time in college. When I attended Union University, I lived with the Jenkins family during the summer and winter semesters. Dr. Jenkins was an internist at the Jackson Clinic and taught Sunday school at Englewood Baptist Church. He was a layman, but he was probably one of the godliest men that I've ever been around. I can still remember the impact he had on me before and just after I was called to the ministry. I would come down in the morning to head out to work in the maintenance crew at the college, and I'd see him on his knees, praying in his office. Every night, they had family prayer time at 9 o'clock, and if you were in the house, you had to join in—whether you wanted to or not. I'll never forget the impact that they had on me as I watched this faithful father teaching his family how to be faithful and full of faith.

Here's the whole point of this passage. Husband/Father: *you* are responsible to God for the faith of your family. You will set the standard. You will determine the course. If you have a strong walk with the Lord, most likely, your family will also. But if you aren't faithful, you can't expect them to be.

I'll tell you, I have a real soft spot in my heart for our mothers who have to get the children up, feed them, and get them to church all by themselves because some big, overgrown junior boy won't take his place at the spiritual head of his house. It breaks my heart to hear our children talk about how much they'd love to see their daddy in church, but he's too busy working or hunting or watching the game or the race. He's too "grown up" to bring them to Sunday school. He's too proud to pray with them, read the Bible to them, and talk to them about Jesus.

Hey, Daddy, listen to me: You have a chance to be heaven's hero around your home. You have an opportunity to make your home an outpost of the kingdom of heaven here on earth. But here's what you've got to remember: it takes a faithful father to build a faithful family.

Let me also give you a warning because if you're not careful, you'll get the wrong idea and get disillusioned, disenchanted, and discouraged as you try to fortify your family with faith.

A FAITHFUL FAMILY ISN'T A FLAWLESS FAMILY

I know you know this, but sometimes it's easy to forget it. There's no such thing as a perfect family. Faithful fathers still have their faults and flaws. Godly mothers still make mistakes, and even the godliest homes have children who go astray.

I don't know of a godlier family than the Graham family. Billy and Ruth Graham are, in my opinion, two of the godliest people who have ever walked the face of the earth. But if you read Billy Graham's autobiography, you'll see even they weren't perfect parents. As a matter of fact, the book recounts the time when Franklin Graham rebelled against his father's faith and influence for years—drinking, doing drugs, smoking, and running around with not-so-godly girls.

Don't get the idea that just because you're faithful in your walk with God and you're faithful in the spiritual leadership of your family, you're never going to have struggles or that your children are never going to stray. The Bible says, "Train up a child in the way he should go, and when he is old, he will not depart from it" (Proverbs 22:6). It doesn't say that they'll never depart; it says when they are old, they won't depart from it. Faithful families are not flawless families.

We see two of the flaws that even faithful families face in the brief biography of Isaac. The first was an internal flaw, and the second was an external flaw. One flaw only God knew about and the other everybody knew about.

Look at the first couple of verses of Genesis chapter 26. Verses 1-3 say,

> *There was a famine in the land, besides the first famine that was in the days of Abraham. And Isaac went to Abimelech king of the Philistines, in Gerar. Then the Lord appeared to him and said: "Do not go down to Egypt; live in the land of which I shall tell you. Dwell in this land, and I will be with you and bless you; for to you and your descendants I give all these lands, and I will perform the oath which I swore to Abraham your father."*

ISAAC: A FAMILY FAITH

God came to Isaac and said, "Don't go down to Egypt." Do you know why God said that? Because God knew Isaac better than Isaac knew Isaac. Abraham had gotten into all kinds of trouble down in Egypt. He'd lied about his wife being his sister, and he picked up a slave girl named Hagar in Egypt. He really had gone "down" into Egypt. And God knew that in Isaac, there was just enough of his father, Abraham, to get him into trouble if he went down there.

And so, God warned him to stay away from Egypt. But even though he didn't go down to Egypt, he still showed that he was his father's son when he lied and told Abimelech that Rebekah was his sister. The apple doesn't fall very far from the tree, does it? He was faithful, but he wasn't flawless.

The second family flaw was a little more evident. Look at the end of chapter 26. Verses 34-35 say, "When Esau was forty years old, he took as wives Judith the daughter of Beeri the Hittite, and Basemath the daughter of Elon the Hittite. And they were a grief of mind to Isaac and Rebekah."

Wait a minute. Isaac didn't raise Esau that way. Isaac had been a one-woman man. And yet Esau went out and started taking multiple wives. He rebelled against the ways and wisdom of his father by marrying these two women, and the Bible says that "they were a grief of mind to Isaac and Rebekah."

All of this is to say that even faithful families have their faults and flaws. There is no such thing as a perfect family. We're all marred by sin. We're all going to fall short. That's not to justify it; it's not to excuse it. There are consequences to our sins that may even be born out in the lives of our children, just like Isaac inherited the family sins of his father, Abraham. But by the grace of God, we can break those sins, bind those sins, and build our family into the family God would have them to be. But here's the great part: even when we're not faithful, we can always remember that God is.

YOUR FAMILY CAN FACE THE FUTURE THROUGH FAITH

Read Hebrews 11:20 one more time: "By faith, Isaac blessed Jacob and Esau concerning things to come." Isaac's faith was firm about the future despite his flaws and failures.

Now look at Genesis chapter 27. This is, in my opinion, one of the most difficult passages in the Bible to determine what *really* happened, what was *supposed* to happen, and *why* what happened happened. (How many of you follow?)

To give you the Whitt's Notes version, what happened was this: Isaac was about to die, and he wanted to give his first son, and really his favorite son, what was called "the blessing." A blessing was half prophecy and half a personal wish from the one giving the blessing. It could only be given once. Once given, it could never be rescinded. This blessing rightfully belonged to Esau since he was the firstborn, but Jacob listened to his mother and deceived his father, and as a result, he received the blessing rightfully belonging to Esau.

Genesis 27:28-29 says, "Therefore may God give you of the dew of heaven, of the fatness of the earth, and plenty of grain and wine. Let peoples serve you, and nations bow down to you. Be master over your brethren and let your mother's sons bow down to you. Cursed be everyone who curses you, and blessed be those who bless you!"

We won't take the time to totally deal with and discuss this tremendous deception, but what we can learn from this twisted tale is that God is totally in control. He knew that this would happen before Isaac asked Esau for some savory meat. He knew this would happen before Rebekah told Jacob how to pull it off. The future is as history to God.

I heard about a college student who went in for a test right before Christmas break, and the professor had only put one question on the test—but it was a doozy. That student looked at it and thought about it but finally gave up and wrote, hoping that the professor would have mercy, "Only God knows the answer to this question. Merry Christmas."

The professor gave the test back with this written at the top: "God got 100. You got a 0. Happy New Year."

CHAPTER SEVEN

JACOB: A PILGRIM FAITH

Hebrews 11:21; Genesis 27-28, 32-33, 48

I heard about a nun who worked for a local home health care agency. As she was out making her rounds one day, she ran out of gas. As luck would have it, there was a station just down the street. She walked to the station to borrow a can with enough gas to start the car and drive to the station for a fill-up. The attendant regretfully told her that the only can he owned had just been loaned out, but if she would care to wait, he was sure it would be back shortly. Since the nun was on the way to see a patient, she decided not to wait and walked back to her car. After looking through her car for something to carry to the station to fill with gas, she spotted a bedpan she was taking to the patient. Always resourceful, she carried it to the station, filled it with gasoline, and carried it back to her car. As she was pouring the gas into the tank of her car, two men walked by.

One of them turned to the other and said, "Now that is what I call faith!"

Through the past several chapters we've been walking and working our way down through this tremendous listing of the faithful to see what lessons we can learn and what characteristics we can glean from these mighty men and wonderful women of the faith.

In this chapter, as we come to Hebrews chapter 11, verse 21, we are introduced once again to a man by the name of Jacob. Recall in a previous chapter where we talked about his father, Isaac, who blessed him and his estranged brother, Esau, "concerning things to come."

In between verses 20 and 21, more than one hundred years have passed, and now Jacob is an old man. He's 147 years old, and he's just about to die. The Bible says in verse 21, "By faith Jacob, when he was dying, blessed each of the sons of Joseph, and worshiped, leaning on the top of his staff."

I had planned on calling Jacob's faith "a quiet faith" because the Bible says in Genesis 25:27 that he was a "mild man" or a "quiet man," Then, as I continued to study Hebrews 11, I thought about calling Jacob's faith "a dying faith" because he was about to die. Then I saw that last little phrase, "leaning on his staff," and I remembered why Jacob had that staff: he was a pilgrim. This was his pilgrim's staff. As a matter of fact, that's exactly what Warren Wiersbe calls it in his commentary on this verse. Look back to verse 13. The Bible says Abraham and his descendants "were strangers and pilgrims on the earth." Of course, according to 1 Peter chapter 2, that's what we as Christians are as well. We are "strangers and pilgrims" (1 Peter 2:11).[17]

Given all of this, I want to refer to Jacob's faith as "a pilgrim faith."

As the old hymn by Albert Brumley says, "This world is not my home, I'm just a passin' through. My treasures are

---

17. Warren Wiersbe, *Be Confident: Live by Faith, Not By Sight (NT Commentary: Hebrews)* (Colorado Springs, CO: David C. Cook, 1982), 147.

laid up somewhere beyond the blue. The angels beckon me from Heaven's open door, and I can't feel at home in this world anymore."[18]

Someone said that a *fugitive* is one running from home. A *vagabond* is one who has no home. A *stranger* is one who is away from home. But a *pilgrim* is one who is on his way home.

As you study Jacob's life, there were three major events—three major spiritual happenings that defined his life. There are some wonderful things we can learn about a "pilgrim faith" from these three major events in the life of this old man by the name of Jacob. Here's the first one.

IT'S BETTER TO WALK THAN RUN

Turn back with me in your Bible, and some one hundred years earlier, to Genesis chapter 27.

Jacob, "the heel-catcher" (that's what his name means), has just tricked his father, Isaac, into giving him the birthright that, by tradition, belonged to his older brother, Esau. Now, remember: Jacob was a mama's boy; Esau was a daddy's boy. Jacob was a homebody; Esau was a bubba. Jacob drove a little electric putt-putt car; Esau drove a big four-wheel-drive pickup truck. Jacob was a tree-hugger; the only trees Esau hugged were the ones that he climbed up with his deer stand. Jacob was a lover; Esau was a fighter. And in Genesis 27, Esau was fighting mad.

Verses 41-44 say,

> *So Esau hated Jacob because of the blessing with which his father blessed him, and Esau said in his heart, "The days of mourning for my father are at hand; then I will kill my brother Jacob." And the words of Esau her older son were told to Rebekah. So she sent and called Jacob her younger son, and said to him, "Surely your brother Esau comforts himself concerning you by intending to kill you.*

---

18. Albert Brumley, "This World Is Not My Home." Public domain.

Now therefore, my son, obey my voice: arise, flee to my brother Laban in Haran. And stay with him a few days, until your brother's fury turns away."

Look down at Genesis 28:10–29:1:

Now Jacob went out from Beersheba and went toward Haran. So he came to a certain place and stayed there all night, because the sun had set. And he took one of the stones of that place and put it at his head, and he lay down in that place to sleep. Then he dreamed, and behold, a ladder was set up on the earth, and its top reached to heaven; and there the angels of God were ascending and descending on it. And behold, the LORD stood above it and said: "I am the LORD God of Abraham your father and the God of Isaac; the land on which you lie I will give to you and your descendants. Also, your descendants shall be as the dust of the earth; you shall spread abroad to the west and the east, to the north and the south; and in you and in your seed all the families of the earth shall be blessed. Behold, I am with you and will keep you wherever you go and will bring you back to this land; for I will not leave you until I have done what I have spoken to you." Then Jacob awoke from his sleep and said, "Surely the LORD is in this place, and I did not know it." And he was afraid and said, "How awesome is this place! This is none other than the house of God, and this is the gate of heaven!" Then Jacob rose early in the morning and took the stone that he had put at his head, set it up as a pillar, and poured oil on top of it. And he called the name of that place Bethel; but the name of that city had been Luz previously. Then Jacob made a vow, saying, "If God will be with me, and keep me in this way that I am going, and give me bread to eat and clothing to put on, so that I come back to my father's house in peace, then the LORD shall be my God. And this stone which I have set as a pillar shall be God's house, and of all that You give me I will surely give a tenth to You." So Jacob went on his journey and came to the land of the people of the East.

Jacob found out that it's a whole lot better to walk with God than it is to run from sin. You see, Jacob left thinking that he only had to outrun Esau, but he quickly discovered that it really wasn't Esau who was chasing him—it was his own sin. His own sin was stalking him. His own deception had dogged his every step from Beersheba to Bethel. And so, worn out and run down, Jacob stopped, settled on a stone for a pillow, fell fast asleep, and began to dream.

There's a lot that's been said and sung about this dream, but most of the time, the focus is all wrong. Most of the time, the focus is either on the ladder or the angels, but if you read the text closely, the main point isn't the angels or the ladder; it's the Lord Himself.

God comes to this heel-catching deceiver and says, "I want to walk with you. I will go with you. I will journey with you." And it was there at Bethel that Jacob received the promise of God and believed the promise of God and stopped running and began to walk with God.

I wonder what you're running from today. I wonder what you lie awake at night thinking of, with your soft pillow feeling like a stone? I wonder what chases you in your dreams. Is it your past—past mistakes, past failures, past sins? Is it your present— the sins that you refuse to give up? Is it your future—the hidden desires that you're planning on following through with?

Maybe you've already determined in your heart this week to cheat on your spouse, cheat on your client, or cheat on that test. Maybe you've already decided you're going to disobey the godly counsel that you've been given. Maybe you've said, "I know what I'm supposed to do, but I'm going to do this instead," or "I'm going to skip out on church," or "I'm going to withhold my tithe," or "I'm going to drop out of this ministry, or that ministry," or "I'm going to ruin this person's reputation," or "I'm going to refuse to forgive that person who hurt me."

Jacob had no idea when he lied to Isaac how far his sin would take him, and if it hadn't been for the grace of God, he'd still be running today. But God showed him grace and offered to walk with him and be his God, and Jacob began to walk with God.

I can still remember what teachers used to yell at me in the hall when I was growing up at K. D. McKellar Middle School, Park Avenue Junior High School, and finally, Milan High School. It was great advice, not just for school but for the Christian life: "Walk! Don't run."

I'll tell you, and I'm speaking from personal experience here: it's a whole lot better to walk with God than to try and outrun your sin.

> *When we walk with the Lord, in the light of His Word,*
> *what a glory He sheds on our way.*
> *While we do His good will, He abides with us still*
> *as with all who will trust and obey.*[19]

You see, just because Jacob was faithful doesn't mean that he was fearless. He was afraid of Esau before, and he's still afraid of him here. The reason Jacob was afraid of Esau was because he thought Esau would do to him what he would have done to Esau if he'd been in his shoes. So, like the great fearless leader that he was, he sends his servants ahead of him with all kinds of gifts and goodies to try and buy Esau's forgiveness, but just in case that doesn't work, Jacob decides to stay behind in the camp and wait until the morning.

What happens next is one amazing story. We're not told how he got there or where he was from. We're told only that,

---

19. John Henry Sammis, "Trust and Obey" in *Hymns Old and New* (1887). Public domain.

> *Jacob was left alone, and a Man wrestled with him until the breaking of day. Now when He saw that He did not prevail against him, He touched the socket of his hip; and the socket of Jacob's hip was out of joint as He wrestled with him. And He said, "Let Me go, for the day breaks." But he said, "I will not let You go unless You bless me!" So, He said to him, "What is your name?" He said, "Jacob." And He said, "Your name shall no longer be called Jacob, but Israel; for you have struggled with God and with men and have prevailed." Then Jacob asked, saying, "Tell me Your name, I pray." And He said, "Why is it that you ask about My name?" And He blessed him there. And Jacob called the name of the place Peniel: "For I have seen God face to face, and my life is preserved." (Genesis 32:24-30)*

This is the second great spiritual crisis in Jacob's life. He'd met the Lord twenty years before at Bethel, but here at Jabbok, Jacob struggled with God and was changed forever. At Bethel, he saw a ladder; at Jabbok, he saw the Lord. At Bethel, he became a believing man; at Jabbok, he became a broken man. At Bethel, he became a son of God; at Jabbok, he became a saint of God. He went away from Bethel with a spring in his step; he went away from Jabbok with a lasting limp.

At Bethel, he died to sin; at Jabbok, he died to self.

DON'T FORGET TO FORGET

Turn to Genesis 48, where you will read the third and final major event in the life of Jacob. This is what Hebrews 11:21 is specifically talking about. Genesis 48, beginning in verse 1, says,

> *Now it came to pass after these things that Joseph was told, "Indeed your father is sick"; and he took with him his two sons, Manasseh and Ephraim. And Jacob*

was told, "Look, your son Joseph is coming to you"; and Israel strengthened himself and sat up on the bed. Then Jacob said to Joseph: "God Almighty appeared to me at Luz in the land of Canaan and blessed me, and said to me, 'Behold, I will make you fruitful and multiply you, and I will make of you a multitude of people and give this land to your descendants after you as an everlasting possession.' And now your two sons, Ephraim and Manasseh, who were born to you in the land of Egypt before I came to you in Egypt, are mine; as Reuben and Simeon, they shall be mine. Your offspring whom you beget after them shall be yours; they will be called by the name of their brothers in their inheritance. But as for me, when I came from Padan, Rachel died beside me in the land of Canaan on the way, when there was but a little distance to go to Ephrath; and I buried her there on the way to Ephrath (that is, Bethlehem)." Then Israel saw Joseph's sons, and said, "Who are these?" And Joseph said to his father, "They are my sons, whom God has given me in this place." And he said, "Please bring them to me, and I will bless them." Now the eyes of Israel were dim with age, so that he could not see. Then Joseph brought them near him, and he kissed them and embraced them. And Israel said to Joseph, "I had not thought to see your face; but in fact, God has also shown me your offspring!" So Joseph brought them from beside his knees, and he bowed down with his face to the earth. And Joseph took them both, Ephraim with his right hand toward Israel's left hand, and Manasseh with his left hand toward Israel's right hand and brought them near him. Then Israel stretched out his right hand and laid it on Ephraim's head, who was the younger, and his left hand on Manasseh's head, guiding his hands knowingly, for Manasseh was the firstborn. And he blessed Joseph, and said: "God, before whom my fathers Abraham and Isaac walked, the God who has fed me all my life long to this day, the Angel who has redeemed me from all evil, bless the lads; let my name be named upon them, and the name of my fathers Abraham and Isaac; and let them grow into a multitude in the midst of the earth." Now when Joseph saw that his father laid his right hand on the head of Ephraim, it displeased him; so he took hold of his father's hand to remove it from Ephraim's head to Manasseh's head. And Joseph said to his father, "Not so, my father, for this one is the firstborn; put your right hand on his head." But his father refused and said, "I know, my son, I know. He also shall become a people, and he also shall be great; but truly his younger brother shall be greater than he, and his descendants shall become a multitude of nations." So he blessed them that day, saying, "By you Israel will bless, saying, 'May God make you as Ephraim and as Manasseh!'" And thus he set Ephraim before Manasseh. (vv. 1-20)

There are a lot of things we could talk about here in this blessing. We could talk about what it means to be adopted as a son of God. We could talk about the providence of God and how God guided this blind old man about to die to make sure that His will be done and make sure that the one who needed to be blessed was blessed. But that's not what I want you to see. *Ephraim* means "fruitful," *Manasseh* means "forgetful." Don't forget to forget.

You say, "Pastor, what are you talking about?" Well, these are Joseph's boys, and Joseph, after all the terrible things that have happened to him—being sold into slavery, being accused of trying to rape Potiphar's wife—he names his son "Forgetful" to show that he has placed all those things behind him. And here's Jacob, who hasn't had nearly as many trials as Joseph, but Jacob can't forget.

Some may say, "I'll forgive, but I'll never forget." Well, really, if you can't forget, you haven't forgiven.

One of the great things about God is that He is able to forget. The Bible says that He can separate our sins as far as the East is from the West, and they'll never meet. He can bury them in the deepest part of the sea of His forgetfulness. God has the ability to forgive. And folks, I am telling you, if you are still holding onto that image in your mind of someone who wronged you, you haven't really forgiven, and you haven't forgotten. You are living in a prison of your own making.

You have two choices when God breaks you. You can get better and be blessed, or you can get bitter. Jacob really hadn't forgotten. It's amazing—we expect God to forgive and forget our sins, but we're not willing to forgive the one who hurt us.

As you travel through this world, people are going to hurt you and do you wrong, and you can carry these around with you and let them weigh you down. But, if you want to know what it means to walk in liberty, forgive and forget.

Now, what can we learn from Jacob's life? It's better to walk with God than it is to run with sin. The greatest decision you can make today is to walk with God. If you don't know Jesus today, won't you begin to walk with Him like Jacob did in Bethel? Walk with God.

You've got to understand that before you can be blessed, you must be broken. And it's how you respond to God's breaking of your pride and will and stubborn, self-sufficient nature that will determine how you live the rest of your life. Will you be blessed, or will you be bitter?

Don't forget to forget. Isn't it great that God forgives our sins? Once you go to him and you repent, once you ask Him to forgive you, God forgets. Shouldn't we do the same?

Here, we are pilgrims without the funny-looking hats and big buckled shoes. Here is Jacob worshipping God as he is about to die, leaning on his shepherd's staff, the same staff he's had with him all those years. He's a pilgrim. He understands that we're just passing through. Don't put all your treasures here. Don't become too invested here. Don't become too tied down to this world because we're just spending the night here.

CHAPTER EIGHT

JOSEPH: A VISIONARY FAITH

Hebrews 11:22; Genesis 37

Over the past several chapters, we've been studying the lives and faith of folks like Abel and Enoch, Noah and Abraham, Sarah and Jacob and Isaac. I've given so much time to these individuals because there was something unique, something genuine, and something special about their faith that prompted the Holy Spirit to pick them out and point them as examples for us to follow today. That is not to say they were perfect; they weren't. That's not to say they didn't, at times, blow it; they did. That's not to say they never tripped up because, as you and I have studied them, we've already seen they had feet of clay just like we do. They were liars/schemers, doubters/deceivers, wonderers/worriers. Sometimes, they got ahead of God, and sometimes, they got away from God, but in the final analysis, these folks possessed amazing faith in the Person and purposes of God.

Faith in faith won't accomplish anything, but faith in God can move mountains. That's why Jesus said in Matthew 17:20-21, "If you have faith as a mustard seed, you will say to this mountain, 'Move from here to there,' and it will move; and nothing will be impossible for you. [Well, how do you have that kind of faith? Jesus tells us.] However, this kind does not go out except by prayer and fasting."

Faith comes by spending time with God. It comes by committing yourself to God. It comes when you trust God more than anything or anybody else in this world. That's what made these folks the giants of the faith that they were. Before the first drop of rain ever fell on this earth, Noah prepared for a flood because God had told him to. Abraham left the only home that he had ever known to live the rest of his life in tents because God had told him to. Sarah started decorating a nursery in her nineties and buying diapers and formula (figuratively speaking) because God told her to. They heard the word of God, and they believed the God of the Word, and as a result, they exhibited and experienced great faith.

In this chapter, we come to one of the most loved and admired characters in the Old Testament. His name is Joseph, and most of us have heard stories about this man all our lives. We've heard about his coat of many colors. We've heard about the wonderful dreams he had. We've heard how he was sold by his brothers to become a slave in Egypt. We've heard how he was lied about and placed in prison, but then, because of his character and commitment to God, God took him from the prison and put him in the palace. He literally went from rags to riches. He was the son of a wealthy father who became a slave, but then, because of his faith and faithfulness, God raised him up to become the number two man in all of Egypt, second only to Pharaoh himself. Here was an extraordinary man with an extraordinary faith. As a result of that, throughout the ages, great men of God have seen in Joseph a type of Christ—a picture of Jesus, if you will.

JOSEPH: A VISIONARY FAITH

Matthew Henry wrote, "His story is so remarkably divided between his humiliation and his exaltation that we cannot avoid seeing something of Christ in it."[20] J. Vernon McGee said, "There is no one in Scripture who is more like Christ in his person and experiences than Joseph."[21]

Now, why do you think that is?

Why do you think that one-quarter of the book of Genesis is given to detail and describe the life of Joseph? (I mean, God dismissed the creation of the universe with five words: "He made the stars also. . ." but He gave over thirteen chapters to this one individual.) Why do you think that so much time and space is given to someone who wasn't even in the Messianic line, like Abraham, Isaac, and Jacob? Why do you think that the Holy Spirit picked this particular person out who so typified the Person and experiences of Christ that no matter which point of his life you point to, some aspect of the Person or work of Jesus will be revealed?

I'll tell you why.

The great goal of the Holy Spirit in the life of any person is to make them more like Jesus. Romans 8:29 says, "For whom He foreknew, He also predestined to be conformed to the image of His Son." God's desire is for you and me to become more and more like the Lord Jesus, and when a person does at last exhibit the beautiful characteristics of Christ, he becomes a trophy of grace that is worthy of a deathless display, an eternal exhibition, in the great gallery of grace just like Joseph.

Look in Hebrews chapter 11, and let's read what the Word of God has to say in verse 22 about this great, godly man by the name of Joseph: "By faith Joseph, when he was dying, made mention of the departure of the children of Israel, and gave instructions concerning his bones."

---

20. Matthew Henry, *A Commentary on the Holy Bible: Genesis to Deuteronomy* (London: The Religious Tract Society, 1836), 94.

21. Taken from *Thru the Bible: Genesis through Revelation* by J. Vernon McGee. Copyright © 1984 by J. Vernon McGee. Used by permission of HarperCollins Christian Publishing. www.harpercollinschristian.com.

What in the world is all of that about? Well, as we're going to see in a minute, Joseph lived a long life. Right before he died, he looked into the future some four hundred years, to a time when his family and their families would leave Egypt and return to the land of Canaan—the Promised Land. Joseph told his family not to leave his bones in Egypt. He wanted his bones carried with them and buried with his father in Hebron. That's why the Bible says in the book of Exodus that when they left, under the leadership of Moses, one of those Israelites had one great responsibility: he was responsible for carrying the bones of Joseph back to the land of Canaan.

Joseph saw the events four hundred years before they happened. He was able to look forward into the future to a time when the children of Israel, the people of God, would leave Egyptian bondage in what has been called "the Exodus."

Ex means "out of."

Odos means "the road or the way or the path."

Joseph saw all of that because he possessed a visionary faith. Now, let me share with you several things we can learn from the faith and faithfulness of this mighty man by the name of Joseph. Here's the first thing.

BIG DOERS ARE BIG DREAMERS

Turn to Genesis 37. In this chapter, we are introduced to Joseph and his "coat of many colors." We are told how his father loved him and how his brothers hated him. Then we're told in verse 5, "Now Joseph had a dream. . . ."

The Bible says Joseph was a dreamer. His brothers even called him that. They said, "Look, this dreamer is coming!" (v. 19). He dreamed big dreams. That's why I say big doers are big dreamers.

Not all big dreamers are big doers, but all big doers are big dreamers. Just look around you, and you'll find this to be true. If you are going to accomplish anything great, you'll have to have a great dream. That's why I want to encourage you to dream big dreams. I want to encourage you today to be a person who dreams big dreams for the glory of God. Parents, you need to tell and teach your children that there's a great big world out there, and they need to have a great vision of what the Lord wants to do through them.

Like one old missionary I heard when I was at Union University said, "Expect great things from God and attempt great things for God."

Now, I want you to listen closely because you aren't going to hear this from the average pastor of the average Baptist church: There are not enough dreamers in the world. There are not enough people who have a God-sized vision in the world, and the Bible says where there is no vision, the people do what? That's right, they perish. You need to have a vision; you need to have a great big dream that God has placed in your heart. That's what Joseph had. He had a God-sized dream because it was a God-given dream.

Notice what the Bible says about this young man's dream:

Now Joseph had a dream, and he told it to his brothers; and they hated him even more. [Can I say this to you? When you have a dream, other people won't like it because most people like to live a dull, boring life. Like somebody said, "Most of our Baptist churches are just the bland leading the bland." Joseph had a dream.] So he said to them, Please hear this dream which I have dreamed: There we were, binding sheaves in the field. Then behold, my sheaf arose and also stood upright; and indeed your sheaves stood all around and bowed down to my sheaf." And his brothers said to him, "Shall you indeed reign over us? Or shall you indeed have dominion over us?" So they hated him even more for his dreams and for his words. Then he dreamed still another dream and told it to his brothers, and said, "Look, I have dreamed another dream. And this time, the sun, the moon [that's a picture of his father and mother], and the eleven stars [that's a picture of his brothers] bowed down to me." So he told it to his faither and his brothers; and his father rebuked him said to him, "What is this dream that you have dreamed? Shall your mother and I and your brothers indeed come to bow down to the earth before you?" And his brothers envied him, but his father kept the matter in mind. (Genesis 37:5-11)

Here's a man who dreamed big dreams, and I want to say it to you again: be a dreamer. Dare to dream big dreams for the glory of God.

Bruce Wilkinson wrote in *The Dream Giver,*

God has placed in the heart of everyone in the world, and especially children, a dream. And when you're young you have that dream, but as you get older people try to take that dream, circumstances try to come and crush that dream, BUT you were put on this earth for a purpose. You're not here to just take up space. You're not here to just be a consumer. You're not here to live and grow old and die. God has a plan and a purpose for your life.[22]

That's why I quote that verse from Jeremiah 29:11 so often. "I know the thoughts I think toward you, says the Lord, thoughts of good and not of evil, to give you a future and a hope."

You see, God has a big purpose for you. It's more than just getting married and having children (although there's nothing wrong with that). There's more to life than just living and taking up space on this earth and then dying as an old person. Hear me today. God has a purpose and a plan for your life, and you need to dream big dreams for the glory of God.

Think about it.

Reading this book could be the person who reaches the last unreached people group in the world with the gospel of the Lord Jesus Christ. Reading this book could be the person God

---

22. Bruce Wilkinson, *The Dream Giver: Following Your God-Given Destiny* (Colorado Springs, CO: Multnomah, Penguin Random House, 2003).

uses to spark the next great awakening. Reading this book could be the next Adrian Rogers, W. A. Criswell, or Billy Graham. Reading this book could be the next Bertha Smith. Reading this book could be the person who opens up North Korea or Iran to the gospel.

I'm telling you, dream big dreams and do big things for the glory of God because big doers are big dreamers, and little thinkers are big stinkers. Which one do you want to be?

PRIDE GOES BEFORE A PIT

You say, "That sounds like Scripture." It is close. Proverbs 16:18 says, "Pride goes before destruction and a haughty spirit before a fall." And, boy, did Joseph have a fall. He was humbled big time. One of the things Joseph struggled with as a young man was pride. To say that he was confident was an understatement. He was proud. He was arrogant. He was cocky.

In some ways, I can see how he got here. He was his daddy's favorite. He was good-looking. The Bible says that "Joseph was handsome in form and appearance" (Genesis 39:6). He was smart. He'd always gotten anything and everything that he wanted. His father even had a beautiful coat made for him to show him that he was his favorite.

And so, in order to humble him and take him down a few notches, God allowed Joseph's brothers to throw him into a pit and sell him as a slave in Egypt. (You can read all about it in Genesis 37:12-24.)

As you read the Bible, one of the things you'll find is that God hates pride. It was because of pride that Lucifer rose up against God and tried to take over heaven. Mark Twain wrote, "A proud man is one who's always looking for a vacancy in the Trinity."[23] I know it's pride keeping a lot of people from accepting Christ. Somebody has well said that "an egotist is a self-made man who worships his creator."

---

23. Mark Twain. Public domain.

I know it's pride that traps a lot of people in their sin. J. Vernon McGee said, "[The greatest] sins of the ministry [are] pride."[24]

I know it's pride that demands its own way. C. S. Lewis said, "There are only two kinds of people in the end: those who say to God, 'Thy will be done,' and those to whom God says, in the end, 'Thy will be done.'"[25]

For those reasons, and maybe for some others, God hates pride. The Bible even uses those exact words in Proverbs 6:16-17: "These six things the Lord hates, yes, seven are an abomination to Him [and then number one, right off the bat]: A proud look. . . ."

If you really want to know what God thinks about pride, just read the book of Proverbs. Proverbs 11:2 says, "When pride comes, then comes shame; but with the humble is wisdom." Proverbs 29:23 tells us, "A man's pride will bring him low, but the humble in spirit will retain honor."

God hates pride, and He will do whatever it takes to purge pride from your life—even allowing you to get thrown into a pit. I'm going to make this one statement, and then I will move on. I was thinking yesterday as I was writing that pride really is the opposite of true faith. Pride trusts the imperfect; faith trusts the perfect. Pride humiliates when it thinks it exalts; faith exalts when it thinks it humbles. Pride is puffed up; faith is filled up. Don't be prideful. Be faithful because pride goes before the pit.

SOME LESSONS CAN ONLY BE LEARNED IN A DUNGEON

For the sake of time, I'm going to make a long story not quite so long. Joseph was thrown into a pit and then sold as a slave in Egypt. He ended up in the house of a man named Potiphar.

---

24. Taken from *Thru the Bible: Genesis through Revelation* by J. Vernon McGee, p. 292. Copyright © 1984 by J. Vernon McGee. Used by permission of HarperCollins Christian Publishing. www.harpercollinschristian.com.

25. *The Great Divorce* by CS Lewis © copyright 1946 CS Lewis Pte Ltd. Extract used with permission.

JOSEPH: A VISIONARY FAITH

Perhaps you know the story. Potiphar was an important and influential man in Egypt. He was the Pharaoh's bodyguard. Joseph rose to such prominence in Potiphar's house that he was made the manager of his master's mansion. One day, Potiphar's wife tried to seduce Joseph and talk him into sleeping with her, but he refused her and said, "How then can I do this great wickedness and sin against God?" (Genesis 39:9). Joseph ran away but left his coat behind. Potiphar's wife ripped her gown, smeared her lipstick, and screamed, "That Hebrew servant tried to rape me! Look, here's his coat!" So Potiphar took him and put him into the prison.

You say, "Great! Joseph did what was right, and for that, he was thrown into prison." But watch, God's not through with Joseph. God's working, and God's shaping, and God's molding Joseph into the man He wants him to be. The Bible says in Genesis 39:21, "But the Lord was with Joseph and showed him mercy, and He gave him favor in the sight of the keeper of the prison."

Look right here. There are some things you and I will never learn in the light of day, and there are some lessons we will only learn in the darkness of a dungeon. My mom had a little saying: "A lesson bought is a lesson taught."

It was in this dirty dungeon that God taught Joseph a lesson he would never forget. In that dungeon, this good-looking, hard-working, intelligent young man finally had to fully place his faith in God's purpose and plan. It was in that dungeon, that prison, that God was molding and making Joseph into the image and likeness of His Son, the Lord Jesus.

Make sure you notice the difference between the pit and the prison. The pit was to punish, while the prison was to perfect. The pit was to chastise, while the prison was to maximize.

Let me tell you something about the Christian life. You can't learn how to live the Christian life from a textbook; you can only learn through time and trials.

Some of you reading this may feel as if you are in prison. You're in a dungeon, and you think God has forgotten all about you. Joseph felt that way. He was stuck in prison for ten years. However, throughout all those years, God never forgot, and God never forsook Joseph. He just wasn't finished with Him yet.

If you're in the dungeon right now, don't despair; remember, there are some things you can only learn when you're there.

YOU CAN'T KEEP A GODLY MAN DOWN

God finished forming and fashioning Joseph down in that dungeon, and then at just the right moment, He brought him before Pharaoh to interpret a repetitive dream.

How many of you know that God is never early, and He is never late? God is always right on time. Well, at just the right time, this dreamer interpreted Pharaoh's dream, and as a result, Joseph, an Israelite, was exalted to the number two position in all of Egypt. He saved the Egyptians from a severe seven-year famine. To show his gratitude, Pharaoh allowed Joseph's brothers, shepherds, to move into the most fertile area in the land, a place called Goshen, becoming the royal flock keepers. The family enjoyed provision and protection for many years because of a godly young man named Joseph.

At the beginning of this story, I mentioned that Joseph is a picture—he's an illustration, a type, if you will, of Jesus. That being the case, I want you to read what the Bible says about the coming and crucifixion and the ultimate coronation of Jesus in Philippians 2:5-11:

> *Let this mind be in you which was also in Christ Jesus, who, being in the form of God, did not consider it robbery to be equal with God, but made Himself of no reputation, taking the form of a bondservant, and coming in the likeness of men. And being found in appearance as a man, He humbled Himself and became obedient to the point of death, even the death of the cross. Therefore,*

JOSEPH: A VISIONARY FAITH

God also has highly exalted Him and given Him the name which is above every name, that at the name of Jesus every knee should bow, of those in heaven, and of those on earth, and of those under the earth, and that every tongue should confess that Jesus Christ is Lord, to the glory of God the Father.

CHAPTER NINE

MOSES: A LIBERATING FAITH

Hebrews 11:23-29; Genesis 2-14

We are quickly approaching the conclusion of our study on the heroes and heroines—the mighty men and wonderful women—who are listed for us here in what has been called *God's Hall of Faith*. In this chapter, we'll make a little transition in our hero's outlook and attitude.

Up to this point, we've been studying idealists. We've been looking at folks who were searching for something ahead of them—something in the future—that would completely change the world that they were living and moving in.

Abel was looking forward to the perfect sacrifice.

Enoch was looking for a life that can only be lived in heaven.

Noah was looking for a reformation and a renovation of a ruined world.

Abraham was looking for a city whose builder and maker is God.

Sarah was looking for the birth of that baby that would fulfill God's promise.

Isaac looked farther down the line than perhaps any of the others and even told his two boys about "things to come."

Jacob was looking forward to being on the other end of that ladder.

Of course, in the last chapter, we saw that Joseph was a dreamer, dreaming of a day when his bones would be carried out of Egypt and buried in the Promised Land.

These were dreamers and idealists. They weren't living for this world; they were living for a world to come. They were looking for something that could only be seen with their spiritual eyes.

In this chapter, we come to a man named Moses; we're not dealing with a dreamer but with a doer. We're not looking at an idealist; we're looking at a pragmatist. We're not dealing with somebody who was only looking for another world with his spiritual eyes; we're dealing with a man who was also looking at this world with his physical eyes. When he did, he saw the evil of Egypt. He saw the sin of society. He saw the plight of his people. He saw the conditions of his countrymen. He had heard the call of the word of God and the cries of the people of God, and he decided to do something about it. One might say, "he put his works where his faith was."

What Moses did is one of the greatest exploits—one of the greatest adventures—in all the Bible. It was so great that it is simply known as "the Exodus." There was even a movie about him that came out many years ago entitled *The Prince of Egypt,* and it is an illustrated story of Moses and the Exodus.

As you study the Bible, you'll discover several things about Moses. First, you'll discover that he was a great man. He was the Lord's great liberator; he led the children of Israel from slavery to freedom. He was the Lord's great legislator; he copied down the Ten Commandments and wrote all five books of the Law. He was the Lord's great leader; he led a rowdy and rebellious bunch of folks on a hiking trip from Egypt to the Promised Land—with just a short detour through the wilderness, which lasted forty years. That's why Acts 7:22 says he was "mighty in words and deeds." He was a great man.

Not only was he a great man, but he was also a meek man. The Bible says in Numbers 12:3, "Moses was very meek, above all the men which were upon the face of the earth." He was *meek*, not *weak*—and there's a big difference. "Meekness is not weakness, but strength harnessed for service."[26] The word *meek* literally means "strength under control."

As you study the book of Exodus, you will find that when Moses was a young man, he was a hothead. He had a terrible temper. He even killed a man with his bare hands and had to run for his life. However, over the next forty years, on the backside of the desert, he learned what it meant to be meek. God saved him, and God changed him to the point where if somebody slapped him, he just turned to God.

Moses was meek, but he wasn't weak. Do you know how I know that? A weak man would never stand before the king of Egypt, Pharaoh himself, and command him to let God's people go. A weak man would never challenge the wizards and wise men of Egypt to a showdown. A weak man would never even start to lead over a million people on a journey across the Egyptian desert toward a so-called "promised land," but a meek man would if God told him to.

The Bible says, "Blessed are the meek, for they shall inherit the earth" (Matthew 5:5). I'd say that the greatest thing that could be said about this meek man, or that could be said about anybody for that matter, is found in Exodus 33:11: "So the Lord spoke to Moses face to face, as a man speaks to his friend."

---

26. Anonymous

Moses spoke to God just like you would talk to a friend across a kitchen table. He was literally on a first-name basis with God. He asked God, "Whom shall I say sent me?" and God said, "You tell them 'I Am' sent you."

Dr. Adrian Rogers used to tell us, "Does God have favorites? I don't believe that God has favorites, but I do believe that God has intimates."[27] And Moses was one of them. The Bible says he spoke to God face-to-face as a man speaks to his friend.

When you study the life of Moses, you'll find that it can be divided into three equal sections, each forty years long.

The first forty years were for education, the second forty years were for preparation, and the last forty years were for proclamation.

The first forty years he spent being a somebody. The next forty years he spent learning to be a nobody. And the last forty years he spent leading everybody.

There are several things I want you to see in this chapter as we talk about Moses and his liberating faith. Here's the first thing.

IMITATION IS THE SINCEREST FORM OF FAITHFULNESS

When reading about Moses's faith in Hebrews 11:23, it's really not his faith that's being talked about there. It's referring to the faith of his parents. Moses had two great, godly parents, Amram and Jochebed, who were great examples, role models, and mentors to him in what it means to love God and live by faith.

---

27. Dr. Adrian Rogers (Love Worth Finding), Sermon: "Knowing God Intimately" (#2150), preached: May 9, 1999. Used with permission.

MOSES: A LIBERATING FAITH

One of the greatest, most practical pieces of advice I could ever give is to make sure you have somebody in your life who is a godly role model, a godly mentor, so you can follow their example and learn to live and walk by faith. Then, you need to be a mentor and a godly example to other people so they can look at your life and say, "That's the kind of life that I want to live for the glory of God." You need to have a mentor, and you need to be a mentor.

Let's look at Moses' life and see what it says about his parents and their godly faith. Hebrews 11:23 says, "By faith Moses, when he was born, was hidden three months by his parents because they saw he was a beautiful child [Of course, have you ever seen somebody who had a baby that they didn't think was beautiful? You know what the old saying says, 'Love is blind.' But, the Bible says that Moses was an usually beautiful baby.]; and they were not afraid of the king's command."

What command are we talking about here? Look back to the first chapter of the book of Exodus, where Pharaoh passed a horrendous law. He declared that all the Hebrew children should be killed. At first, it was just the male children, but later, it was all of them. Boys and girls alike were to be taken and thrown into the crocodile-infested Nile River, where they would either drown or be eaten—or most likely both.

Moses was born under a death sentence, and he was so beautiful that his parents said, "We are not going to let him be killed. We're going to hide him for three months, and we are going to trust God." Their faith drowned out their fear. Their eyes were on a greater King than Pharaoh.

So they made that little basket—the Bible calls it an "ark"—and they put Moses out in the Nile River, trusting that God would protect him.

Look in Exodus 2:1-10. It tells us about Moses' parents here.

HEROES

And a man of the house of Levi went and took as wife a daughter of Levi. So, the woman conceived and bore a son. And when she saw that he was a beautiful child, she hid him three months. But when she could no longer hide him, she took an ark of bulrushes for him, daubed it with asphalt and pitch, put the child in it, and laid it in the reeds by the river's bank. [How does God save a person who is condemned to death? That's what Moses' parents must have asked themselves. Then they remembered Noah and his ark. They remembered that "Noah prepared an ark for the saving of himself and his family" and so they said, "That's exactly what we'll do. We'll make a little ark and we'll put Moses in the river just like Pharaoh commanded, but we'll put him in the ark first. We'll put the ark in between him and the waters of death, and we'll trust God to do for Moses what He did for Noah." So, they put him in that ark and laid him in the river.] And his sister stood afar off, to know what would be done to him. Then the daughter of Pharaoh came down to bathe at the river. And her maidens walked along the riverside; and when she saw the ark among the reeds, she sent her maid to get it. And when she had opened it, she saw the child, and behold, the baby wept. [Here's the favor of God.] So, she had compassion on him, and said, "This is one of the Hebrews' children." Then his sister said to Pharaoh's daughter, "Shall I go and call a nurse for you from the Hebrew women, that she may nurse the child for you?" And Pharaoh's daughter said to her, "Go." So, the maiden went and called the child's mother. Then Pharaoh's daughter said to her, "Take this child away and nurse him for me, and I will give you your wages." [She got paid for nursing her own baby.] So, the woman took the child and nursed him. And the child grew, and she brought him to Pharaoh's daughter, and he became her son. So, she called his name Moses, saying, "Because I drew him out of the water."

Moses had godly parents, and what an example of faith to him they were. John Phillips writes, "They were made of the stuff of martyrs."[28]

Let me tell you something: you and I need godly examples of faith to follow. We need to have those who love God and live for God, who can be role models we can imitate and teach us how to grow in our faith. The Bible says in Hebrews 13:7, "Remember those who led you, who spoke the word of God to you; and considering the result of their conduct, imitate their faith." Paul said, "Therefore I urge you, imitate me" (1 Corinthians 4:16).

You may be reading this and thinking, *Well, Pastor, you have godly parents you could follow. You were raised in a Christian home, but I don't have godly parents like Moses did.* Listen, you may not have godly parents, but if you need a godly pattern to follow to imitate their faith, God's already given you godly examples if you'll just look around. In your church, there are godly deacons, godly teachers, godly men, and godly women whom you can look to as examples of faith to imitate and grow in your walk with Jesus.

I not only want to encourage you to find somebody and imitate their faith; I want to encourage you to be the kind of Christian other people can imitate and follow your example of faith. You be a godly example for someone else because imitation is the sincerest form of faithfulness.

YOU DON'T HAVE TO WALK LIKE AN EGYPTIAN

All the Boomers and X-ers will know where that came from. Moses was born in Egypt, raised in Egypt, and even lived in Egypt, but Moses was not an Egyptian. One might say, "he was *in* Egypt, but he wasn't *of* Egypt."

---

28. Taken from *Exploring People of the Old Testament*, vol 2, p. 14 © Copyright 2006 by John Phillips. Published by Kregel Publications, Grand Rapids, MI. Used by permission of the publisher. All rights reserved.

Read what Hebrews 11:24-25 says: "By faith Moses, when he became of age, refused to be called the son of Pharaoh's daughter, choosing rather to suffer affliction with the people of God than to enjoy the passing pleasures of sin."

Let's be honest. Some pastors would have you think sin isn't fun and there's no pleasure to it. Listen, the devil's smarter than that. If it wasn't fun, nobody would do it. Like somebody said, "To err is human, but it feels divine."

The problem is not that sin isn't fun—it is. It's just that once you sin, you become a slave to sin. Jesus said: "Whoever commits sin is a slave of sin" (John 8:34). You get to enjoy sin, and then sin gets to enjoy you.

I heard about two country boys who lived way up in the Smokey Mountains, back where the zip code is EIEIO. One day, they spotted a bobcat up in a tree and decided to have some fun. One of the boys looked at the other and said, "I'll shimmy up that there tree and chase him down to you, and you grab him and put him in a sack." So, he climbed up the tree and grabbed ahold of the limb the bobcat was sitting on. He shook it and jerked it back and forth until that old bobcat fell to the ground. The other fella grabbed it and tried to put it in the sack, but the bobcat had other plans. There was a terrible fight. There was screaming and crying and clawing and scratching. Dust and hair and fur and skin were flying in every direction. The fella who had climbed up in the tree hollered down, "What's the matter? Do you need help catching one little old bobcat?" In between screams and cries, his friend hollered back, "No, I don't need help catching him; I need help letting him go."

How many of you know how that feels? One of Scripture's greatest but most neglected truths is that once you are in Christ, you are no longer a slave to sin. Now, before you are saved, you don't have a choice—you will sin. If you're reading this book and you're lost, you will sin. You can't get around it.

MOSES: A LIBERATING FAITH

You can't get away from it. Without Jesus, you will sin. You don't have a choice. Jesus told a bunch of Pharisees one day, "You are of your father the devil, and the lusts of your father you will do" (John 8:44). You'll sin every day, and you'll sin in every way. You don't have a choice.

Once you are in Christ, the Bible teaches that you can choose not to sin. Oh, you can still sin. You still have the ability. You're still in a fallen, sinful body with sinful desires and habits, but the difference is that you don't have to sin. Now you have a choice. That is the glorious difference of being in Christ and Christ being in you. You no longer are a slave to sin. You've been liberated. You've been set free. Now, you can do like Moses—you can choose to live a holy life instead of a hellish life. Moses chose "rather to suffer affliction with the people of God than to enjoy the passing pleasures of sin" (Hebrews 11:25).

I don't know if you know this, but at the end of the Civil War, after the war had been fought, a president had been assassinated, and an amendment to the Constitution had been signed into law, setting free all of those who had once been in slavery, amazingly there were still those who chose to live in slavery. They still chose to live in the same squalor and the same situation they had before the Emancipation Proclamation. They were free, but they chose to live as enslaved people.

Listen. You don't have to live like a slave. You don't have to walk like an Egyptian. You don't have to live in bondage to sin. You can choose today to live a life of liberty in the Lord Jesus Christ.

This fact brings up a crucial question. How can you live a liberated life? You've got to be born by the spirit. John 3:6 says, "That which is born of the flesh is flesh, and that which is born of the Spirit is spirit." If you're in the flesh, you will do the works of the flesh; you don't have a choice. But if you're of the spirit, you will begin to exhibit the fruits of the spirit. You've got to walk in the spirit. Galatians 5:16 says, "Walk in the Spirit, and you shall not fulfill the lust of the flesh."

Have you ever wondered why you sometimes stumble and fall back into sin? That's because you're not walking in the spirit, and when you're not walking in the spirit, that old carnal, fleshly nature will begin to rise up, and you've got to beat it back down again. You've got to be led by the spirit. Galatians 5:18 says, "But if you are led by the Spirit, you are not under the law." Second Corinthians 3:17 says, "Now the Lord is the Spirit; and where the Spirit of the Lord is, there is liberty." The second thing we learn from looking at the liberating faith of Moses is you and I don't have to walk like Egyptians.

IT'S BETTER TO FEAR GOD THAN MAN

Look at Hebrews 11:27:

> *By faith he forsook Egypt [By the way, that's what faith is all about: forsaking all and trusting Him. Egypt is a picture of the world, and if ever the world put on a great disguise and tried to make itself attractive, it did so for Moses. It offered him everything on earth. It offered him social position. It offered him sinful pleasures. It offered him staggering prosperity. But, because of the great faith that he learned from his godly parents, Moses' faith triumphed over all of these worldly delights and He became one of God's intimates. Moses could have had it all. He could have had anything and everything that he wanted, but instead he gave up the gold of Egypt and got the God of heaven. He forsook the king of Egypt to follow the King of heaven. He chose a life of godly sacrifice over a life of gilded splendor. He gave up the opportunity to be a king to become a slave. He rejected this world and received heaven. That's what faith is all about. He*

forsook Egypt], not fearing the wrath of the king; for he endured as seeing Him who is invisible.

Psalm 111:10 says, "The fear of the Lord is the beginning of wisdom." Do you want to know what ultimately made Moses the mighty man of faith that he was? Do you want to know why he became one of God's intimates—literally, he was the only man to see God with his own eyes? Here's the difference: Moses cared more about what God thought than he did about what Pharaoh thought. He cared more about what God said than he did about the commands of Pharaoh. He feared God, and he loved God more than Pharaoh.

I've said it before, and I'll say it again: If you please God, it doesn't matter who you displease, and if you displease God, it doesn't matter who you please. Just make sure you please God; He'll cause even your enemies to be at peace with you. It's better to please God than man.

BELIEVE AND LIVE; REJECT AND DIE

Look at Hebrews 11:28-29; you will see that is precisely what we are taught: "By faith, he kept the Passover and the sprinkling of blood, lest he who destroyed the firstborn should touch them. By faith they passed through the Red Sea as by dry land, whereas the Egyptians, attempting to do so, were drowned."

We're looking at faith here, and these were two instances where faith was a matter of life and death. These were two instances where the Israelites had to trust God totally to live. They had to believe and live or reject and die. Now, that's a principle that you'll find throughout Scripture: life comes by believing God, and death comes by rejecting Him. You can either believe what God says and experience life, or you can reject the Word of God and experience death.

For those of you who don't know Jesus and have never given your heart to Christ, God is saying to you, "Trust me.

Believe me. Accept me. If you do, you'll experience not just life but abundant life." Jesus told us that if we reject Him, we will experience not only physical death but, ultimately, spiritual death. Believe and live; reject and die.

Moses believed, and Moses lived, and Moses led the children of Israel all the way to the edge of the Promised Land, where God took him up on a mountain and rocked him to sleep and buried him with His own hands. He had been God's personal, intimate friend, and God would not have had it any other way. Moses had a liberating faith, and you and I can experience that same kind of faith today.

Frederick Douglass grew up in slavery in Maryland during the early nineteenth century and experienced its brutality. He was taken from his mother when he was only an infant. For years, as a child, all Douglass had to eat was runny cornmeal dumped in a trough that kids fought to scoop out with oyster shells. He worked in the hot fields before sunup until after sundown. He was whipped many times with a cowhide whip until blood ran down his back, he was kicked and beaten by his master until he almost died, and he was attacked with a spike by a gang of whites.

Even so, when Frederick considered escaping to freedom, he struggled with the decision. He writes in *Narrative of the Life of Frederick Douglass: An American Slave* that he had two great fears. The first was leaving behind his friends whom he loved more than his own life, for he thought that friendship's bond was stronger than slavery's pain. His second fear was that if he failed, his future as a slave would be solidified.[29]

Today, people who find themselves in slavery to sin and who think about escaping to freedom in Christ may have similar fears. They may fear leaving behind friends. They may fear they'll fail in their attempt to break from sin and live free for God. They should take heart from Douglass's experience.

---

29. Frederick Douglass, *Narrative of the Life of Frederick Douglass: An American Slave*, originally published in 1845 (New York: Cosimo, Inc., 2008), 63.

On September 3, 1838, he remembered the following: "I left my chains and succeeded in reaching New York without the slightest interruption of any kind; I have been frequently asked how I felt when I found myself in a free State. It was a moment of the highest excitement I ever experienced. I felt like one who had escaped a den of hungry lions."

Two thousand years ago, another liberator came out of Egypt. The Bible says in Matthew 2:15 about Jesus, "That it might be fulfilled which was spoken by the Lord through the prophet, saying, 'Out of Egypt I called My Son.'"

CHAPTER TEN

RAHAB: A SAVING FAITH

Hebrews 11:31; Joshua 2

This chapter concludes our series on the mighty men and wonderful women listed for us in *God's Hall of Faith*. Throughout this book, I have prayed that you wouldn't just learn about faith but begin to walk by faith as you have watched and learned from people like you and me.

I wrote at the beginning of this book, and I'll reiterate it here at the end. We often get the impression that the people we read about in the Bible were super-spiritual people with super-spiritual powers that enabled them to do things you and I will never be able to do. However, as we've studied them, I hope you've seen they were folks who were a lot like you and me. They had their good days and their bad days. They had days when they walked with God, as well as days when they ran from God. There were times when they obeyed and times when they disobeyed. There were times when they believed and times when they doubted. Nevertheless, when it had all been boiled down, when the fat was in the fire, and when the rubber hit the road, they simply trusted God to do what He said He would do.

Faith is simply trusting God.

To recap where we've been and what we've learned from our heroes, let me remind you that in Hebrews chapter 11, we are given the definition, description, and demonstrations of real faith. The *definition* is found in verse 1, where the writer of Hebrews says, "Now faith is the substance of things hoped for, the evidence of things not seen." The *description* is found in verses 2-3, which says, "For by it the elders [that's all the folks that we've been looking at and learning from] obtained a good testimony. By faith we understand that the worlds were framed by the word of God, so that the things which are seen were not made of things which are visible." Finally, the *demonstrations* are what we've been studying throughout this book.

At the beginning of this book, I gave you a simple, working definition of real faith. Faith is hearing, believing, and acting on the Word of God. Again, it is taking God at His word despite the situation or circumstances. That's why Paul wrote in Romans 10:17, "So then faith comes by hearing and hearing by the word of God." That's why Paul wrote in 2 Corinthians 5:7, "We walk by faith, not by sight."

In this final chapter, we are introduced to the final person named in Hebrews chapter 11. We are given the ultimate example of what faith can do in a person's life. You see, nature forms us, sin deforms us. The world conforms us, but faith transforms us.

Oh! What a transformation took place in the life of a wicked, worldly woman named Rahab. Look at Hebrews 11:31, and let's read about the fantastic faith of this former fallen female, Rahab: "By faith, the harlot Rahab did not perish with those who did not believe when she had received the spies with peace."

In Joshua chapter 2, we are introduced to a shady lady named Rahab—a prostitute who lived in a pagan city called Jericho. For history buffs, Jericho is the oldest city in the

RAHAB: A SAVING FAITH

world; no other city was built before Jericho. For geography buffs, it's the lowest city in the world. It sits right at the top of the Dead Sea, the lowest point on the planet. So here we have a pagan prostitute living in the oldest and lowest city on the face of the fallen world. That is a picture of sin if there ever was one. Rahab was a pagan living in spiritual darkness. She was a prostitute living in spiritual depravity. She was a person facing sudden destruction. Yet she experienced physical and spiritual salvation because she found grace through faith.

Dr. Warren Wiersbe says that God was gracious in His salvation of Rahab—a Canaanite condemned to die. Although He commanded the destruction of the city of Canaan, God showed mercy to Rahab, a Gentile—a real example of Ephesians 2:1-10.[30]

Rahab is one of the most incredible pictures in the Old Testament of what salvation can do in a person's life. She was a harlot who became a hero. She was a citizen of Jericho who became a citizen of heaven. She was a shady lady of Jericho who became a shining star for the Jewish people. She was a lady who had slept with the most perverted of Jericho, who later married a prince of Israel. She was so changed and transformed that she became the great-great-grandmother of King David. She was so changed and transformed that she became part of the bloodline from which the Messiah, Jesus Christ, would be born.

Matthew chapter 1 provides the lineage of Jesus, the baby who would be born in Bethlehem to save the world from their sins. Verse 1 begins,

> *The book of the genealogy of Jesus Christ, the Son of David, the Son of Abraham: Abraham begot Isaac, Isaac begot Jacob, and Jacob begot Judah and his brothers. . . [You get the idea, so look down at verse 5.] Salmon begot Boaz by Rahab, Boaz begot Obed by Ruth, Obed begot Jesse, and Jesse begot David the king. . . And Jacob begot*

---

30. Dr. Warren Wiersbe, *The Bible Exposition Commentary*, vol 1 (Colorado Springs, CO: Victor—Cook Communications Ministries, 2003), 26.

Joseph the husband of Mary, of whom was born Jesus who is called Christ. (vv. 1-2, 5-6, 16)

To see what the gospel's transforming power can do in a person's life, look at Rahab. She's come a long way from being a pagan prostitute to being an ancestress of the Messiah! That's why Romans 5:20 says, "But where sin abounded, grace did much more abound."

It is essential for us to remember that Christ came into this world to save sinners. First Timothy 1:15 says, "Christ Jesus came into the world to save sinners, of whom I am chief." Review Joshua chapter 2 and see what the Bible says about Rahab's saving faith.

Now Joshua the son of Nun sent out two men from Acacia Grove to spy secretly, saying, "Go, view the land, especially Jericho." So, they went and came to the house of a harlot named Rahab and lodged there. [There's evidence right here of her faith. She took her life in her hands the moment that she allowed those spies to come into her home and hide.] And it was told the king of Jericho, saying, "Behold, men have come here tonight from the children of Israel to search out the country." So, the king of Jericho sent to Rahab, saying, "Bring out the men who have come to you, who have entered your house, for they have come to search out all the country." Then the woman took the two men and hid them. So, she said [watch her; she's about to lie], "Yes, the men came to me, but I did not know where they were from. [That's a lie.] And it happened as the gate was being shut, when it was dark, that the men went out. [That's a lie.] Where the men went, I do not know [That's a lie.]; pursue them quickly, for you may overtake them." (vv. 1-5)

All my life, I've heard church folks say, "Well, I know I told a little white lie, but after all, Rahab told a lie too." Hey,

RAHAB: A SAVING FAITH

Rahab didn't just tell one lie; she told several, and she also did a lot of other things.

> *(But she had brought them up to the roof and hidden them with the stalks of flax, which she had laid in order on the roof.) Then the men pursued them by the road to the Jordan, to the fords. And as soon as those who pursued them had gone out, they shut the gate. Now before they lay down, she came up to them on the roof, and said to the men: "I know that the L*ord *has given you the land, that the terror of you has fallen on us, and that all the inhabitants of the land are fainthearted because of you. For we have heard how the L*ord *dried up the water of the Red Sea for you when you came out of Egypt, and what you did to the two kings of the Amorites who were on the other side of the Jordan, Sihon and Og, whom you utterly destroyed. And as soon as we heard these things, our hearts melted; neither did there remain any more courage in anyone because of you (Now, watch it, here's her profession of faith. Here's how we know that she was saved.), for the Lord your God, He is God in heaven above and on earth beneath." (vv. 6-11)*

Wow! What a profession of faith from the lips of a lady whose life had been lived imprisoned to pagan idolatry and public immorality. She believed in one God, not the multitudes of gods that populated the pagan temples. She believed in a personal God who would work on behalf of those who trusted Him. She believed He was the God of Israel who would give the land to His people. He was not limited to one nation or land but rather was the God of heaven and Earth. Rahab believed in a great and awesome God and had placed her faith in Him.

> *"Now therefore, I beg you, swear to me by the* Lord, *since I have shown you kindness, that you also will show kindness to my father's house, and give me a true token, and spare my father, my mother, my brothers, my sisters,*

and all that they have, and deliver our lives from death." So, the men answered her, "Our lives for yours, if none of you tell this business of ours. And it shall be, when the LORD has given us the land, that we will deal kindly and truly with you." Then she let them down by a rope through the window, for her house was on the city wall; she dwelt on the wall. And she said to them, "Get to the mountain, lest the pursuers meet you. Hide there three days, until the pursuers have returned. Afterward you may go your way." So the men said to her: "We will be blameless of this oath of yours which you have made us swear, unless, when we come into the land, you bind this line of scarlet cord in the window through which you let us down, and unless you bring your father, your mother, your brothers, and all your father's household to your own home. So it shall be that whoever goes outside the doors of your house into the street, his blood shall be on his own head, and we will be guiltless. And whoever is with you in the house, his blood shall be on our head if a hand is laid on him. And if you tell this business of ours, then we will be free from your oath which you made us swear." Then she said, "According to your words, so be it." And she sent them away, and they departed. And she bound the scarlet cord in the window. They departed and went to the mountain and stayed there three days until the pursuers returned. The pursuers sought them all along the way but did not find them. So the two men returned, descended from the mountain, and crossed over; and they came to Joshua the son of Nun, and told him all that had befallen them. And they said to Joshua, "Truly the LORD has delivered all the land into our hands, for indeed all the inhabitants of the country are fainthearted because of us." (vv. 12-24)

I want us to discover three tremendous truths as we examine Rahab's saving faith. Here's the first one.

RAHAB: A SAVING FAITH

YOUR PAST DOES NOT DETERMINE YOUR FUTURE

Look back at Hebrews 11:31. The Bible says, "By faith the harlot Rahab. . . ." Some folks are defined by their occupations. *Dr. So-and-So. Judge So-and-So. Reverend So-and-So.* And that is evidently the case with Rahab. As a matter of fact, in the days when Joshua's spies snuck into Jericho, her job was practically her last name. *Rahab the harlot. Rahab the prostitute.*

You see, in those times, there were two types of prostitutes. The first were the religious ones who worked in the temple. Then, there were the average, ordinary, run-of-the-mill prostitutes who worked wherever they could. Rahab didn't work at the temple. Some might even say she ran a brothel. There have been those who have tried to say Rahab was just an innkeeper. And no doubt, her establishment, situated so closely to the city gates of Jericho, had often served many a weary traveler. The only difference was that for the price of clean sheets, a guest found a woman waiting between them.

Here is the amazing thing: Hebrews 11:31 tells us, "Rahab did not perish with those who did not believe, when she had received the spies with peace." Rahab isn't remembered for her harlotry but for her bravery. She isn't remembered so much for her profession as for her confession. She isn't remembered for loving men but for trusting God.

Yes, she had a sordid past, but because of her faith and the transformation it brought to her life, she was blessed with a godly husband named Salmon, a prince of Israel, and an honorable son named Boaz. If that was not enough, she was placed in the greatest listing of the faithful in all the Word of God—not because she deserved it but because God was faithful and reached out in grace to her and transformed her life forever.

That's exactly what God does for us. We don't deserve it—that's why it's called "grace" (**G**od's **R**iches **A**t **C**hrist's **E**xpense).

God reached out to us and offered us the greatest gift anyone could ever receive: the forgiveness of all our sins.

As of this writing, some of you have already started putting up your Christmas decorations and playing holiday music in your car, house, or at your desk. Think of it this way: We have a great big, gorgeous gift with our name on it. God's gift of salvation. All we have to do is receive it.

But that's the problem some of you are having—accepting the gift. You're having a hard time getting past all the sin and the shame that's in your life and believing God has forgiven you. You need to get past the past. If you've received Jesus, placed your faith in Him for salvation, asked Him to forgive you of your sins, then He already has. You have been transformed. You've been changed. The Bible says in 2 Corinthians 5:17, "Therefore, if anyone is in Christ, he is a new creation; old things have passed away; behold, all things have become new." That's why you can pitch your tent and camp out on Romans 8:1, which says, "There is therefore now no condemnation to those who are in Christ Jesus, who do not walk according to the flesh, but according to the Spirit."

Rahab placed her faith in Yahweh, the Lord God, and because of her faith, she experienced and enjoyed the same transformation you can experience today. You see, the first thing we learn from Rahab is that your past does not determine your future.

Here is the second truth that we learn from Rahab.

A PERSONAL DECISION LEADS TO A PUBLIC CONFESSION

Think back to the scarlet cord that Rahab hung outside her window. I am sure she had hung ropes out that window many times before so husbands could escape from a wife who had found out or so some politician could evade an angry citizen.

We know Rehab lowered the spies down from her place by a rope. But this wasn't a rope; it was a cord, and there was a big difference. Some even translate it as "a ribbon." If you'll notice, she tied it to the window just as soon as those two spies' feet hit the ground. Destruction was coming, and she wasn't taking any chances.

I want you to think about that scarlet red ribbon momentarily. The moment Rahab tied that ribbon, that cord, to her window, she was a marked woman. She was marked as a sinner to all the children of Israel because she was identified as the harlot who had helped them. But she was also identified as a traitor to all of Jericho. Oh, they may not have realized it at the time, and by the time they figured it out, it wouldn't have mattered, but she still took a big chance by flying that red ribbon so everyone would know which side she was on. That's why I say true saving faith can't be hidden for long.

As you hold this book, consider Rahab. Like her, you've placed your faith in Jesus. You've been transformed. You've been changed, and even though it may mark you as a sinner, even though it may seem traitorous to some of your friends, what you've got to understand is that a personal decision always leads to a public confession. Psalm 107:2 says, "Let the redeemed of the Lord say so, whom He has redeemed from the hand of the enemy." Jesus said it even more straightforwardly: "Therefore whoever confesses Me before men, him I will also confess before My Father who is in heaven. But whoever denies Me before men, him I will also deny before My Father who is in heaven" (Matthew 10:32-33).

Here's the last truth we learn from Rahab's saving faith.

A FAITH DEMONSTRATED IS A FAITH DECLARED

Rahab believed in God, received God's grace, and took a stand on God's side. She was accepted into God's people and even placed into the lineage of the Son of God. She's cited as an example of faith in Hebrews 11 and given as an example of works in James chapter 2.

So that leaves us with the $24,000 question: Why?

I'll tell you why. Rahab put her works where her faith was. She put her life where her love was. She demonstrated what it means to have a saving faith, and because of her demonstration, her faithfulness has been declared to all generations.

Now, I want to go straight for the goal and explain what it means to have a saving faith. A saving faith is a personal faith placed in a powerful God to change you from the inside out and prepare you for eternity. It comes when you realize you have sinned against a holy God. Rahab had, and Rahab did.

Next, you must ask that powerful, personal God to forgive you of your sins. Rahab did that.

Then, you accept Him as Lord and Savior and acknowledge Him before men. That's the whole point of Rahab's story, and that's what it means to have a saving faith.

Since the beginning of this book, I have looked forward to and thought about this chapter. I can't think of a better picture for us to have in mind—of a sinner who experienced God's great salvation—as we look back with thanksgiving and look forward to celebrating the birth of the Savior. After all, that's why He came. Matthew 1:21 says, "And she will bring forth a Son, and you shall call His name Jesus, for He will save His people from their sins."

I don't know about you, but one of my favorite Christmas carols is "The First Noel." The fourth verse contains a tremendous statement of salvation theology you may never have noticed.

Then let us all with one accord,
sing praises to our heavenly Lord;
that hath made heaven and earth of naught,
and with His blood mankind hath bought.[31]

---

31. "The First Noel," first transcribed in 1823 in "Some Ancient Christmas Carols" (London). Public domain.

UNWAVERING OBEDIENCE

Hebrews 11, the cornerstone of faith in the Bible, holds immense significance. This chapter, guided by the Holy Spirit, provides us with faith's very essence, depiction, and manifestation. Exploring the faith of these biblical figures offers profound insights into what genuine faith looks like. Each of them demonstrated a unique aspect of faith that made them stand out as heroes and heroines of the faith.

Abel's faith is highlighted by his sacrificial offering that pleased God (Genesis 4:4; Hebrews 11:4). He showed faith by offering his best to God, demonstrating a heart that sought to honor and please Him.

Enoch walked with God, showing an intimate and consistent faith (Genesis 5:22; Hebrews 11:5). His faith was characterized by a close relationship with God, resulting in a life that pleased God so much that he didn't experience death but was taken by God.

Noah's faith is evident in his obedience to build the ark (Genesis 6:22; Hebrews 11:7). Despite ridicule and opposition, he obeyed God's command, showing unwavering trust in God's Word.

Abraham and Sarah's faith is highlighted by their willingness to believe God's promise of a son despite their old age and barrenness (Genesis 15:6; Hebrews 11:8-12). Their faith was marked by trust in God's faithfulness and the fulfillment of His promises.

Isaac, Jacob, Moses, and Joseph continued this legacy of faith, each in their way, trusting God despite challenges and uncertainties.

Rahab's faith stands out because she, a Gentile and former prostitute, trusted in the God of Israel and protected Israelite spies (Joshua 2:9-11; Hebrews 11:31). Her faith led to her salvation and inclusion in the lineage of Jesus Christ (Matthew 1:5).

The common thread among these individuals is their unwavering trust in God, even when faced with difficult circumstances or uncertainty. Their faith wasn't just about belief but was demonstrated through action. They trusted God's promises and obeyed His commands, even when it seemed irrational or impossible. By studying their faith, we can learn valuable lessons about what it means to trust in God wholeheartedly and live a life pleasing to Him. Their examples encourage us to live lives of faithfulness, obedience, and trust in God's promises, even when the world around us may challenge our beliefs.

ADDITIONAL BOOKS BY DR. BRAD WHITT
& INNOVO PUBLISHING

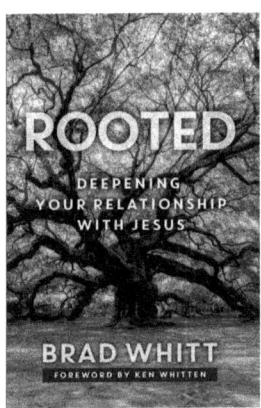

Rooted: Deepending Your Relationship with Jesus

Those who are rooted in Christ are equipped to withstand the storms of life—like the wise man that built his house on a rock and was not "tossed to and fro and carried about with every wind of doctrine" (Eph. 4:14). They will find nourishment in Christ and peace that surpasses understanding.

God's will for every believer is that they abide in His will and have absolute confidence in their salvation. With that confidence, we can be *Rooted* in our God-given purpose.

40 Days of Refreshment: Quiet Times for Hectic Hearts

There is only one place we can find the spiritual refreshment that will enable us to live the life that Jesus desires for us: the Word of God.

40 Days of Refreshment is a devotional to guide you in your walk with Jesus. The number 40 represents more than just a time of testing—it represents teaching. Moses learned what it meant to walk with God, the lessons proving vital when he stood before Pharaoh to speak for the "I AM." The Israelites learned important life lessons in their wilderness wanderings. Do you think Noah ever again doubted the promise, protection, or provision of God? Even Christ's forty days in the desert with the devil set the stage for the greatest ministry that the world has ever known.

www.ingramcontent.com/pod-product-compliance
Lightning Source LLC
Chambersburg PA
CBHW070505100426
42743CB00010B/1761